Essays
In
Modern
American
Literature

GENERAL EDITOR: RICHARD E. LANGFORD
Stetson University

ASSOCIATE EDITORS: GUY OWEN
North Carolina State University

WILLIAM E. TAYLOR
Stetson University

STETSON UNIVERSITY PRESS
DeLAND, FLORIDA

STETSON STUDIES IN HUMANITIES NO. 1

Essays In Modern American Literature

COPYRIGHT 1963 BY STETSON UNIVERSITY

MANUFACTURED IN THE UNITED STATES OF AMERICA FIRST EDITION

For Spook

To help him build an elephant

Contents

AMERICAN CHARACTER IN AMERICAN LITERATURE:
AN ACCEPTANCE OF EXPERIENCE
John Hague • 1

SOME CONTRAPUNTAL THEMES IN HERMAN MELVILLE
W. Hugh McEniry • 14

HIGH IDEALS AND CATCHPENNY REALITIES IN
HENRY JAMES'S *The Portrait of a Lady*
David W. Marcell • 26

STEPHEN CRANE AND THE GIANT VOICE IN THE
NIGHT: AN EXPLICATION OF *The Monster*
Sy Kahn • 35

IMAGERY AND MEANING IN *The Great Gatsby*
Guy Owen • 46

ETHICAL POINT OF VIEW IN *The Sound and the Fury*
Robert J. Griffin • 55

EUGENE O'NEILL: THE MASK OF ILLUSION
Richard E. Langford • 65

STEINBECK'S WINE OF AFFIRMATION IN
The Grapes of Wrath
J. P. Hunter • 76

TENNESSEE WILLIAMS: ACADEMIA ON BROADWAY
William E. Taylor • 90

THAT WAS NO LADY — THAT WAS JACK KEROUAC'S GIRL
Eliot D. Allen • 97

JAMES GOULD COZZENS: A CULTURAL DILEMMA
Richard P. Adams • 103

THE QUAKING WORLD OF JAMES PURDY
Warren French • 112

PREFACE

These essays have not appeared in print before; they are fresh, original, critical comments on major American authors. Most of the essays are the contributions of experienced, active teachers of American literature, offering the student and general reader literary criticism of scholarly depth, written informally. I think there is much in the collection that should be available outside of college classrooms, and I hope others will think so, too.

I am heavily indebted to my two associate editors, Guy Owen and William E. Taylor, who read and offered valuable comments on each essay submitted. They kept me from making many mistakes. More important, they believed in my purpose when sometimes I did not.

Richard E. Langford
Stetson University
January, 1963

• JOHN HAGUE *took his Ph.D. in American Studies at Yale, and is now Head of the Department of American Studies at Stetson University. His articles have appeared in several academic journals.*

*American Character in
American Literature:
An Acceptance of
Experience*

IT IS NOT DIFFICULT to understand why the Germans, who were defeated in the first World War and were confronted with economic problems which threatened to liquidate an entire way of life, should have experienced a feeling of radical despair. A German doctor, writing to an American lawyer in the 1930's, attempted to explain his seemingly implausible support of Adolph Hitler. The lawyer insisted that Hitler's promises were irrational and that his treatment of the Jews was barbaric. The doctor readily admitted the charges, but asked his friend to consider the alternative. The alternative to belief was nonbelief, and nonbelief put daily life into a context in which it was simply and totally without meaning. Unless he could believe in the fascist miracle, the doctor added, his daily decisions would become irrelevant to the real problem of human existence.

It is a little more puzzling, perhaps, to explain the threat of meaninglessness which pervades so much of America's creative literary and artistic endeavors in the past several decades. To be sure, one can cite the disillusionment of war, the experience of a great depression and a growing sense of alienation as factors which in some fashion have undermined the traditional security of the American people; and these things are real enough. One can go a step further and point to the combination of technological and industrial factors which have recreated the outlines of a corporate society without establishing a genuinely meaningful community that would lend the corporate image substance. This explanation is closer, I think, to the heart of the matter and deserves fuller attention than I propose to give it in this essay.

What I wish to examine in some detail, however, is a tradition in American thought and letters which not only reflects American character but which illuminates much of our present anxiety and restlessness. My contention is that American literary expression has been consistently shaped by the manner in which it has consciously or unconsciously come to terms with its own immediate past. Further, it has been victimized in the 20th century by a past which it could neither accept nor repudiate.

Thomas Jefferson was one of the first who denied a cumbersome role to the American past. When he observed the salutary effects of an occasional revolution, he was merely expressing his conviction that every generation was entitled to the same opportunities enjoyed by its predecessor. His belief that no government should borrow money which it could not repay in a single generation likewise affirmed that everyone was entitled to a fair start.

Jefferson's fair start did not imply that the past was without relevance. His own love of traditional literature, as well as his efforts to revive classical architecture, suggest that he made good use of numerous historic traditions. Moreover, when he enumerated Newton, Bacon and Locke as the three greatest men who ever lived, he was testifying to his belief in the cummulative growth of knowledge, and that deliverance from ignorance and superstition depended on just such an accumulation. Properly understood, therefore, the past was an asset. Only when traditions denied equal opportunity were they to be ignored or set aside.

In a special sense, however, Jefferson was insisting upon the need for meeting the present on its own terms. The concept of agrarian self-sufficiency implied confidence about the happiness which would accrue to those who utilized each new opportunity to the full. In this regard Franklin was more typical than Jefferson. Practical, self-educated Ben constantly gave the impression that he was equal to the task of furnishing new solutions for new problems, and of providing a more comfortable way of life in the bargain. It is not surprising that Americans have considered him representative of the national character. His attitude and intellectual posture suggest change and growth: they suggest confidence about the results of disciplined, empirical techniques, and they imply that the doors are open to all who meet the present on its own terms.

Later, Emerson and his Concord friends intensified these demands on the present moment. They sought a mystical experience which, while illuminating the past, also rendered it in a peculiar sense irrelevant. Emerson's "transparent eyeball" signified that in discovering the oversoul, one also achieved complete comprehension of those forces which animated all great men throughout history. One did not study the past, therefore, to enrich the present in a Jeffersonian sense, but rather to achieve identity with the forces which had shaped previous great creations. The purpose of each moment, as Emerson put it, was "to convert life into truth."

Yet Emerson never could deny the relevance of past experience. As Perry Miller has suggested, he and his friends grappled constantly with the sober truth that their own creative ability was sharply limited by their restricted cultural experiences. Small wonder that they urged each other to ignore their own limitations, and to create a bonafide American literature. Small wonder, too, that Whitman's appearance should have excited both their admiration and their envy.

Whitman's achievement, of course, lay in his great celebration of the triumph which the American, "this new man," had wrought in a magnificent continental setting. Whitman was passionately alive to the whole panorama of

American landscapes and experiences. He agonized over its failures, prophesied its growth, and hymned the whole in the manner of one who constantly converted life into truth.

Henry James also took a turn at describing the new man. For example, in *The American*, Christopher Newman (whose very name is suggestive), however lacking in sophistication, possessed the confidence of the self-made man. His life was manageable and seldom oppressive. Newman's past experiences fortified his confidence that the times were not out of joint and that society must ultimately yield to the individual who possessed the requisite strength, talent and will. Thus James' American hero appeared on a stage which he expected somehow to dominate. Unencumbered by tradition, alive to the possibilities of the present, and cheerful beyond 20th century comprehension, Newman filled the present moment with integrity and decisiveness.

In *The American*, the contrast between Newman and the aristocratic Bellegardes is revealing. Madame de Bellegarde, matriarch of the clan, embodies a tradition of substance. Her will is indomitable and her pride inexorable. Her younger son, in a manner suggesting awe, tells Newman that his mother is very strong. Yet the tradition cannot be transmitted. The elder son acquires the form but not the substance, and the younger son and daughter, while grasping the substance recognize that the forms have become archaic. The latter recognize in Newman something they both admire and envy. Like them he is alive; unlike them his talents seem designed for the world in which he lives.

Newman expects change and adjusts readily to it. His measurements of success are worldly and practical. When Madame de Bellegarde feels compelled to remind him that she is very proud, Newman responds immediately that he is "very rich." For Newman the only test of worthiness is how one responds to the present moment. He grants others the privilege of responding in their own way, provided they too respond as self-reliant individuals. Thus he is always, by his own standards, "kind." The one thing which he cannot comprehend is the event in which people respond in terms of tradition rather than self-will. That Valentin should die in a duel or that Claire should enter a convent were in themselves reprehensible. Both Valentin and Claire express to Newman a sense of shame regarding their mother's failure to honor his suit. That the old lady's failure—her transgression—might require expiation on the part of her children was totally beyond Newman's conception of responsibility.

R. W. B. Lewis, in *The American Adam,* has pointed out that Henry James, Sr. believed in the efficacy of a so-called "fortunate fall." It was, according to this concept, necessary for an individual to encounter evil in order to measure his previously acquired strength and endurance. With this notion Henry James, Jr., fully agreed. Before Christopher Newman began his European sojourn, his experience had been completely trustworthy. He could explain in a rational and orderly way the causes of each success and failure, and he possessed as a result the manner and ease of a genuine aristocrat. When Madame de Bellegarde informed him that her daughter had "given him up," she confronted him for the first time with a situation which would not yield to the talents he possessed. The problem thus posed always fascinated James. How *would* the American react when confronted by an unmanageable situation? He could not, in any case, erase the fact of his involvement. The memory would become part of the experience, and a wider range of responses would become available to him.

It was Mr. Newman's merit, as one aristocratic Frenchwoman put it, that he was incapable of idle pleasantries. He was always himself and he was never defensive. Ironically, as America reached industrial maturity at the turn of the century, conditions emerged which placed most successful industrialists on the defensive in a rather startling fashion. This is an old story and scholars have chronicled in detail the reasons for its development. Yet one must give special emphasis to the fact that in the years following the Civil War the exploitation of American resources permitted the growth of large fortunes under circumstances which opened an unprecedented gulf between rich and poor. Again, the story is a familiar one. What often remains unsaid is that the situation which existed in 1900 with respect to income distribution is without parallel in American history. Americans in the Gilded Age had momentarily permitted themselves to believe that the virtues of a competitive struggle for existence negated the equalitarian facets of their tradition. Under such circumstances the benefactors of this transformation sought to justify their position by an appeal to absolute laws in biology, history, economics, and religion. Eric Goldman has aptly referred to these rationalizations as a "steel chain of ideas" which conservatives fashioned to preserve the status quo.

One of the great intellectual watersheds which separated the 19th and 20th centuries was the growing awareness of scholars in the 20th century that all men act upon preconceptions. The realization that absolutes, when applied to the social order, were almost always rationalizations, transformed almost every academic discipline. It is perhaps unfair to compare this growing sophistication to the "fortunate fall," but in the broadest sense the comparison has validity. In the field of history, for example, the naive belief in progress which characterized 19th century scientific history was challenged by an awareness of the relativity of all knowledge. Belief in progress was not demolished, to be sure, but the seeds of a thorough-going skepticism were at least sown.

Morton White has designated the intellectual transformation which scholars accomplished in the first two decades of the 20th century as "the revolt against formalism." It is clear, at the outset, that the revolt was first and foremost a revolt against 19th century absolutes. It is equally clear that the revolt was enormously stimulated by men such as Beard, Veblen, and Dewey, who taught that the social order could be transformed by intelligent leadership. The antiformalists wanted to "liberate" Americans from a false addiction to the past, to narrow the lag between technological and social change, and to solve the problem of inequality. And although they were in one sense revolutionaries, they were in another merely extending 19th century ideas of progress and mission. Moreover, their revolt had behind it an intellectual security which reflected the military security their nation enjoyed. Dewey could afford to do without metaphysics precisely because the Jeffersonian metaphysic upon which he relied seemed, as indeed it had to the sage of Monticello, "self-evident."

In similar fashion Lincoln Steffens could write effectively about *The Shame of the Cities* because the remedy for urban discontent required little analysis and exegesis. Similarly, Samuel Gompers could spell out the precise reforms which organized labor required in order to come of age as a vital institution. Moreover, Gompers could state, by 1917, that Congress had provided every one of the necessary reforms. In short, not only had society agreed with his contentions, but it had managed to act upon them. The final step, passage of the literacy test for immigrants, had been accomplished over Wilson's veto.

Miraculously intellectuals found themselves in the progressive era at the center of events which seemed likely to redeem "the promise of American life." As they outdid one another in reminding colleagues that literature, history, art, economics, sociology, or what have you must be related to *life,* and that scholars and creative artists alike must contribute to the effort which was required to transform society, politicians responded in kind by welcoming aboard the intellectuals to the domain of party and even machine politics. A New Jersey politician approaching the home of Princeton's President Woodrow Wilson was overheard to remark, as he passed through the picturesque garden, "Can you imagine anybody dumb enough to give up this for politics?" But give it up he did—he and numerous academicians like him. For their part the academic historians nominated an amateur historian and professional politician to be the President of their guild, the American Historical Association. He was none other than the hero of San Juan Hill, Theodore Roosevelt.

The "revolt against formalism" was therefore a revolt against Victorianism but not against romanticism. One can even argue that the rebels also incorporated in their arguments what Carl Becker has termed a "double distillation of Puritanism." Although many of them would have been horrified by such a description (but not all of them), it is clear that, in good Puritan tradition, the standard bearers of the revolt spoke for the aroused conscience of the community, and also that they were in hot pursuit of their own version of the Heavenly City. One need only remember the extent to which visions of a socialist utopia fascinated writers such as Jack London and Upton Sinclair, or the extent to which a reform novelist such as Winston Churchill succeeded in romanticising the whole progressive movement, to realize just how indebted to the 19th century the rebels really were. When Wilson sounded the call to duty few reformers doubted that a political honeymoon was at hand.

From the vantage point of 1960 there seems little doubt that the reformers were entirely conscious of their desire to break the "steel chain of ideas" which enveloped late 19th century conservatism. They were also conscious of the fact that they were deploring the loss of economic opportunities and that in some vague way they were protesting the prevalence of gentility and mediocrity. They were much less aware of the extent to which their efforts were tainted with nostalgia. Alfred Kazin's book, *On Native Grounds*, has provided a memorable portrait of Frank Norris in which he suggests the image of an "overgrown boy alternating between Kipling and Zola." At the height of his protest Norris could not conceal his admiration for the man who dared to sieze and wield power, nor his idolization of a way of life that belonged to an agrarian rather than an industrial society. One is tempted to suspect that many of these critics and writers simply did not want to pay the price which advancing technology and mechanization demanded. Given the development of informed, educated citizens, they felt sure that society would advance straight toward the humane goals for which they yearned.

Randolph Bourne was one of the first to sense the problem. When John Dewey announced his general support of America's war effort in 1917, thus abandoning his earlier pacifism, Bourne's fury knew no bounds. Astutely he recognized that Dewey's relativism had been effective as a reforming instrument only because the ends for which he struggled were defined implicitly, but nevertheless absolutely, in the context of American experience. When circumstances demanded that the ends themselves be evaluated, Bourne roared, Dewey and his disciples were as helpless as new born babes.

In an essay entitled *The Dilemma of Diderot,* Carl Becker went a step beyond Bourne. He questioned whether any writer, scholar, or politician, regardless of how carefully he analyzed ends and means, could modify significantly the direction in which his civilization was moving. Diderot, an 18th century philosopher, had argued for a science of natural rights in an effort to discredit the authority by which the kings had preserved their power in the *ancien regime.* The concept of natural rights depended upon the existence of natural laws, however, and Diderot wondered whether the king could not argue as effectively as his opponents that he, not they, was the proper spokesman for these very laws. How could one get around Pope's dictum that "whatever is, is right"? One could get around it by adopting a relativistic position, but in that case one had to be prepared to face the possibility that an opponent's decision, backed by adequate force, might prove to be historically correct.

As Becker considered America's plight in the 1920's and 30's, he found Diderot's problem devastatingly alive. The reformers, he realized, had destroyed the 18th century concept of determinism but had at the same time replaced it with a cultural determinism that cruelly blunted the cutting edge of their relativistic assault upon conservatism's "steel chain of ideas." Now man was discovered to be a product, or indeed a victim, of his environment. It made little difference that some were born in more favorable environments than others; all were so much a part of their culture that none could do much to change it. Like Voltaire they could only "cultivate their gardens."

It required tough-mindedness of a high order to cope with such a crisis. Justice Holmes showed his mettle when he declared that while he was willing to fight for his convictions, truth, in any ultimate sense, would have to be defined by "the majority vote of that nation which could lick all the rest." Only those who were confident about their own strength and capacity would find Holmes' world attractive. In any case, if might made right, 19th century illusions about progress and peace were dead. Stephen Crane, Theodore Dreiser, and others, while perhaps not fully conscious of the intellectual framework which Becker had defined, were acutely sensitive to the possibility that life was an enormous trap.

Perhaps Becker's analysis is merely an indication that American history caught up with the American people in the 20th century. Americans had always been limited by their history and environment, but circumstances had obscured the precise nature of those limitations. In the 19th century Americans had struggled with their physical environment and the land yielded to their demands. The past appeared in the American consciousness merely as a useful foundation upon which to build. After the first World War many Americans suddenly felt victimized or doublecrossed by a past which they had not made — the War came as an enormous shock to most Americans. Wilson had insisted that America must stay out of the War in order to bring to the peace conference standards of neutrality and rationality. When he found that war could not be avoided, he urged the American people to make one final, desperate gamble that they could make the World community rational. The War, therefore, became an ultimate weapon for peace. When Americans awoke in the 1920's to the fact that the tensions unleashed by war could not so easily be dispelled, their disillusionment was severe.

Americans, as a result, inherited from the War the beginnings of a new attitude toward their own past. They found themselves living in a world which was in some respects irrational and unmanageable, and from the standpoint of a people who had demanded so much from the future, such an idea amounted to an earthquake. From the standpoint of the scholars and writers who chronicled the new developments, the earthquake was made more severe by virtue of the fact that their own immediate past stemmed from a period of rebellion and skepticism. Unlike the men who led the "revolt against formalism," these critics had little inclination to feel nostalgic about an idyllic past. What they remembered were dreams and hopes which appeared now only to mock and depress them. Reaction drifted in on a rising tide of normalcy, and although a Mencken might find comfort in satire, the more characteristic response was a growing sense of helplessness and alienation.

Scott Fitzgerald, Eugene O'Neill, John Dos Passos, Robinson Jeffers, Ernest Hemingway, and a score of lesser novelists and playwrights, testified to a sense of despair and a fear that life was without meaning or purpose. Homer Smith, a biologist, tried his hand at novel writing, and in *Komongo,* succeeded in summing up the mood of the "lost generation." Man, thought Smith, must realize not only that he was nature's child, but also that, like other species, he could not guarantee the preservation of his kind. Already the signs pointed to a growing specialization which clearly indicated that man's fate would be the fate of the once mighty dinosaur. Humanism was man's colossal conceit; naturalism was the only philosophy worthy of a mature individual.

To many, it seemed as if the human race had suddenly entered something akin to the Marabar Caves, described in

E. M. Forster's *A Passage to India*. One heard in the caves a mysterious echo that reduced everything from life to death, from happiness to sorrow, to one weird sound—"ouboum." The "lost generation" had no past which it could accept and no hope for the future. Its alienation was real and virtually complete. Here then was the point at which American writers experienced in full measure the fall which Henry James had foreseen.

Two groups have attempted to make their way back from the Caves. One group has sought an answer in the form of existentialism. These people feel that American literature at its best has involved an awareness of the present and a sensitivity to the immediate environment. Ironically, many of them resemble Valentin Bellegarde, who knew he was alive, but had to struggle desperately to prove it, because the substance of the code by which he lived had lost so much of its relevance. Such writers are descendents of the lost generation; their spokesman is Jack Kerouac and their prophet is Karl Shapiro. Their tragedy lies in their attempt to extend into the 20th century the very facet of 19th century experience which is most vulnerable to 20th century conditions. They refuse to see that what gave meaning to the existential writings of their predecessors was their real and viable hopes for remolding the future. And so they demand something from the present which the present cannot give. Indeed the present exhausts itself in endless, mad dashes across the continent.

The second group has attempted something at once more modest and viable. At the end of *All the King's Men*, Robert Penn Warren has Jack Burden tell the reader that he and his wife have discovered that they must accept the past in order to be able to hope for the future. This, it seems to me, is the watchword for writers like Warren, William Faulkner, and T. S. Eliot. They recognize that to them has fallen the task of building a literary tradition in tune with past limitations and future expectations. It is not a criticism of their work, or of American Culture, to suggest that, if the future does not appear as bright to them as it did to Emerson and Whitman, this may be a reflection of the fact that the future *cannot* be as bright as these worthies deemed it. The task is to see if we can live constructively in such a world and perhaps be faithful to the best of our past.

At least our writers have passed through the fire, as James foresaw, and although one suspects at times that Americans surrender innocence just as often as they stop smoking, still the future may offer some hope of fulfilling James' cautiously optimistic expectations.

STETSON UNIVERSITY

- *Educated at Birmingham Southern College and Vanderbilt University,* HUGH McENIRY *is now Dean of Stetson University. Herman Melville was the subject of his doctoral dissertation and his interest in that writer has remained keen during the twenty years he has taught at Stetson.*

Some Contrapuntal Themes in Herman Melville

The question of meaning plagues every man at one time and another. Try as a man will to avoid them, the riddles of his origin, destiny, and significance interrupt his most comfortable moments to nag him for his neglect of them. When self-doubt and insecurity threaten, these same problems add their weight to the heavy burden of his fears. Little men seem to find satisfactory answers most readily, and perhaps for that very reason are deemed little men. Great men wrestle with the fundamental issues at nearly every turning of their lives, because they are great men, and see through the plausible superficiality to the mask behind which reality lies still hidden and unexplained. Herman Melville was one of these latter, as Sophia Hawthorne must have sensed before she wrote, shortly after meeting him, "I am not sure that I do not think him a very great man."

Occasionally — and it is true in the case of Herman Melville — the rest of us are lucky enough to sit in on the dialogue between a perceptive and inquiring man and his world, as he seeks to determine whence he came, where he is going, and whether it makes any difference. There is real reason to believe that Melville never wrote anything that did not address itself somewhat to his consuming search, and that all his works record his investigations into possible solutions of the puzzle of his existence. Indeed, because of the scope of his searching, and because of the totality of his involvement, we come to accept him as a character in the books he wrote, though we do not find him there by name. His imagined worlds, and his daily times and spaces merge until we read Herman Melville as we read his writings; and we understand that neither the man nor the books are complete alone.

This essay, however, will not pretend to examine the whole body of Melville's writing. I shall leave aside such implicit seeking as lies behind his quizzical juxtaposing of civilization and savagery in *Typee* and *Omoo*. I shall neglect, also, for want of space, the important chapters in his story represented by the other novels, the short pieces, and his poetry. It is my thesis here that the grand outline of a lifelong probing into the purport of his existence confronts us in the four statements Melville published in *Mardi* (1849), *Moby Dick* (1851), *Pierre* (1852), and *Billy Budd* (1924). I propose further to show that Melville's explorations brought him two conflicting understandings of man's proper manly reaction to a thwarted effort to comprehend his universe and his place in it. These two understandings, with variations, are the contrapuntal themes weaving in and out of the central focus in each of these novels.

The first of these themes, the one Melville always hoped would turn out to be consonant with reality, affirms that by some form of exertion man can discover the ultimate truth about himself and his world. The second theme makes the claim that man's best chances in this life lie in an expedient adjustment to day-to-day necessities, and a rejection of the lure of absolutes. The meaning he wanted was never revealed to him, and the meaning he recognized as most probably accurate he could not live with happily. He might well have agreed with Camus that the question of suicide is the only valid philosophical issue. But he could not have claimed that there was any joy for him in the grim absurdity he discerned.

Mardi is the confident and determined statement of a young man. The record has to show failure in the protagonist's search; but we cannot help but feel that Taji — and Melville — have been surprised by defeat, and that they do not accept it as final. Melville's energy seems unflagging and his expectations of ultimate success high, despite Taji's apparent setback.

Melville wrote this book shortly after his marriage and establishment in New York City. He was something of a literary lion, and a newly accepted member of the assured little circle around the Duyckinck brothers. His mental and spiritual life prospered under fresh stimulation, too; and he was beginning to read his way through the New York Society Library and the fine private collection of the Duyckincks.

In the midst of all these strange ideas and people, and fascinated by them, he had begun a third novel about the South Seas to follow *Typee* and *Omoo*. It got away from him, and he launched instead into this first of his extended efforts to write out through his books his own concept of the significance of man in the universal drama that looked comic, melodramatic, and tragic by turns. What had commenced as a simple romance about the search of a sailor named Taji for a maiden whom he had rescued from trouble and had then lost becomes something entirely different. On the slender plot line of Taji's search for Yillah, Melville strings a serving of satire, philosophizing, and social criticism — all of it emerging as a by-product of Taji's quest for Ultimate Truth, which Yillah symbolizes.

When it was done, he had to admit that the pure elixir of existence had escaped him. He probably felt, also, that he had eliminated some widely approved possibilities, and narrowed his search for the future. But if he imagined that he had finished with any of the alternatives offered Taji, he came very soon to know that he was in error. Two of the options held out to Taji, and urged upon him as proper substitutes for the last elusive truth about the world and its inhabitants, were to form the second major theme of all his work. At the end, the secondary theme was to become primary.

The dominant theme in Mardi concerns itself with Taji's search for final truth, his rebuff at every turn, and his heroic insistence that he will accept nothing less than infinite understanding itself. The two options he perceives make a strange pair; one pressed him to religious faith, the other to sensuous forgetfulness. Both of the alternatives are, of course, less than perfect rational comprehension as Melville sought it; and both are therefore penultimate solutions to the problem he set himself. Both represent, also, compromises aimed at electing what seems possible rather than demanding what seems impossible; and both are therefore expedient. The contrapuntal play of themes expressive of Melville's yearning for the Absolute, and of his reluctant admission of the wisdom of expediency governs the organization of his life's work.

Babbalanja, the philosopher, makes the claim for Christianity as the most advisable acceptance for a man in this world. He, along with the king, the poet, and the historian who have been companions to Taji in his voyaging, submits himself to the teaching of Alma (Christ). Babbalanja speaks for them all: "My voyage is ended. Not because what we sought is found; but that I now possess all which may be had of what I sought in Mardi [the world]."

Queen Hautia entreats Taji to embrace another expedient. She, too, rejects the possibility that man in his finitude could ever comprehend the infinite truth. She suggests, as did Babbalanja, in his way, that what she has to offer is all that man can know. She proposes the sensate solution, and represents to Melville the temptation for man to forego everything else for gratification of appetite as the highest good, to enthrone the present pleasure above all the past and all the future. Hautia teases Taji:

'Come! let us sin and be merry . . . Ah, Taji! for thee, boot-
less deep diving . . . but join hands, and I will take thee
where thy Past will be forgotten; where thou wilt soon learn
to love the living, not the dead.'

The dominant theme in *Mardi* is that of the search.
Clearly, Melville, with his hero Taji, still anticipates the discovery of a role for man in his world that will be grand
indeed. Taji responds to his friends and to Hautia, finally,
with the same rejection, and sets out from the safe harbor
to pursue his quest: "Now I am my own soul's emperor; and
my first act is abdication! . . . and turning my prow into the
racing tide, which seized me like a hand omnipotent, I dart-
ed through." The tension has been established never to
lessen.

Three years and two novels later, Melville invited his
readers to a second report on the results of his hunt for
meaning in his life — and in ours. He had not neglected his
search in this interval. Particularly in *White Jacket* he had
made some notes on the nature of his progress. In fact, he
closed that book with a plea to his fellow men not to turn
on each other in their voyage through the world, but to trust
that somehow — though no man can know exactly how —
there must be a purpose. This tone is much subdued from
that in which he closed *Mardi*. But for the most part *Red-
burn* (1849) and *White Jacket* (1850) were concerned with
other matters. In *Moby Dick,* Melville came again to the
search for ultimacy and the hateful necessity to settle for less.

Melville's masterpiece is a book full of faults that have
been transmuted into virtues by the power and breadth of
the novelist's concepts, and by the overriding excellence of
the whole despite the weakness of some of the parts. One of
these faults arises from the greater intensity of the counter-
play between Melville's two major themes. There are two
protagonists in *Moby Dick*: Ahab, as the hero of man's magnificent quest for the Absolute; Ishmael, as the prudent ex-
ponent of the attainable.

Ahab, the mighty captain, holds the stage for the greater

part of the novel. His monomaniac hatred of the white whale brings the *Pequod* and its crew to destruction. He will not compromise, scorns expediency, and asks no quarter of infinity. In the wings, having been displaced early in the history by Ahab, Ishmael comments on the increasingly frantic efforts of his captain. When Ahab boasts his strength and will, Ishmael names him maniac. When Ahab renounces every aid but what he can find in his own depths, Ishmael remarks on his fatal pride. And when Ahab and his last command sink in the ocean, it is Ishmael who survives to tell the story.

The two protagonists view the great whale as symbolic of the Infinite they must both confront, but they perceive the problem of this confrontation in different lights. To Ahab, Moby Dick

> . . . swam before him as the monomaniac incarnation of all those malicious agencies which some deep men feel eating in them, till they are left living on with half a heart and half a lung.

To Ishmael, Moby Dick represented ". . . the heartless voids and immensities of the universe . . . a colorless, all color of atheism. . . ." To Ahab came at least the warmth of a specific reply to his announcement that he existed. As long as reply came, even though cruel and punishing, Ahab could believe that a relationship could be founded and maintained. To Ishmael, there was only the bleak knowledge that the "heartless voids" would dispose of him and his kind without ever even being aware that he and his kind had once pitiably existed. The nobler theme of Ahab's faith in man's possibility dominates *Moby Dick,* but the counter theme in which Ishmael counsels a cautious regard for the advisable is heard triumphant at the end.

Thirteen months separated the appearance of *Moby Dick* from the publication of *Pierre,* brought out by Harper and Brothers in November, 1852. In this book, the Ishmael theme, the theme of wary expediency, rises to a crescendo; but the story of Pierre Glendinning is not the tale of an expedient man. Where Taji had entered zestfully upon the search for Infinite Truth, and where Ahab had striven to come to grips with Infinity itself, Pierre attempts to identify with Infinity and come to terms with it. He makes all his crucial decisions with the intent to follow the dictates of the highest and noblest within him. He examines his soul and tries to assure the purity of his motivation in his undertaking. The end of his endeavors is a museum of horrors. He commits incest, murder, and finally suicide. He ruins all who are closest to him, and utterly destroys himself before he takes his own life. *Pierre* is a novel about the honest effort of a man to make his actions acceptable to Infinity's absolute pattern. But its conclusion is negative; in spite of the hero's defiance at the end, the work gives inverted approval to the contrapuntal idea with which we have become familiar, that of expediency.

Pierre does not accept the evidence that his own experience forces him to confess is overwhelming. Despairing and bitter he says:

> 'It is ambiguous still. Had I been heartless now, disowned, and spurningly portioned off the girls at Saddle Meadows, then had I been happy through a long life on earth, and perchance through a long eternity in heaven! Now, 'tis merely hell in both worlds. Well, be it hell. I will mold a trumpet of the flames, and, with my breath of flame, breathe back my defiance!'

Another answer had long been available to Pierre. He had found it in a fragment of a pamphlet supposedly written by Plotinus Plinlimmon. The sheets of paper were in the coach that bore Pierre from one life to another, as he gave up a pattern he had thought to be right for him to answer the call of the moral law he heard in his innermost soul. But the pamphlet said: "A virtuous expediency, then, seems the highest desirable or attainable earthly excellence for the mass of men, and is the only earthly excellence that their Creator intended for them." The counterpoint became starker than it had been before. Pierre fails more abysmally than his predecessors, and the countertheme is stated more strikingly.

It is a curious thing that this sharpening of the struggle between the two themes may not have been entirely conscious on Melville's part. *Pierre* suffers from such great deficiencies in characterization, plotting, and style that the skeleton of its concepts becomes more prominent than it might have in a better executed work.

For nearly forty years after *Pierre,* Melville produced, in the novel form, no further bulletins on the status of his search for meaning. Tantalizing bits of evidence may be found in his shorter pieces. *Israel Potter* and *The Confidence Man* tell us nothing that Melville had not already reported, though the latter does indicate a continuing resistance to expediency as the proper philosophy for man to adopt. For a while, Melville reflected his seeking only in a few lyric poems, and once at great length in the poem *Clarel.* The last book he wrote was another novel recounting some change in his attitudes toward the themes he had explored over nearly half a century. *Billy Budd* was not found until long after Melville died; it was published in 1924.

Melville had never been satisfied with the direction in which his search seemed to be leading him. Steadily, throughout his books, he had scorned the theme of expediency, had insisted that it could not be sufficient, had urged his characters and his readers not to accept it as final—but had in all honesty been impelled to keep it in view as a reasonable alternative to the interpretations he preferred but could not establish as correct. Finally, in *Billy Budd,* the protagonist is the expedient man; the hero bodies forth the maligned penultimate acceptance that Taji would have none of, that Ahab spurned magnificently, and that Pierre equated with baseness.

Each of these men had been ruinously confuted in his struggle to maintain another—and to him better—possibility for man. Taji did not find Yillah for all his diligent and devoted search. Ahab did not slay the white whale. Pierre proved unable to live his life by the chronometric standards of heaven. Woven into the fabric of each tragic failure had been a disdained countertheme, and Melville turned to it at the end. Even then, he made one last effort to uncover a more acceptable alternative.

If man could not search out infinite truth for his guide; if he could not in his own strength strike through all barriers to wrest truth from the infinite; if he could not identify himself with truth in obedience; might he triumph vicariously, after all, in the existence of innocence? Could it be that some blessed men might survive this life without the dawning experience that made Melville's quest necessary? The answer of *Billy Budd* is a sad and final negative. Billy Budd must die, says Melville, as innocence always must in this world; for innocence is not equipped to traffic with experience safely. Nor can men of compassion protect in others the innocence they have forfeited in themselves. Man's essential condition requires innocence to become experience and perish, and to do so without ever really knowing why.

In *Billy Budd* the relative positions of the two themes are reversed. Poor Billy cannot even be the protagonist of his pathetic story. The heroic central figure, for the first time in Melville's major work, is the man of expediency, Captain Vere. The novelist was no happier with the conclusions he had reached than he had been when he first saw the possibility nearly fifty years earlier. But he had sought always to get all the truth he could about man. His last novel had to be consistent with that search.

Captain Vere, obligated by law and circumstance to direct the death by hanging of the young sailor he feels to be innocent of wrong, is the agonized instrument through whom Melville announces that his deepest questionings have brought him only to the rueful confession that expedient action is the wisest action. Captain Vere recognized the pull of the higher law, as did his subordinates sitting as members of Billy's court martial. He, too, wanted to respond to that absolute he felt within him. But he knew—as Melville had come to know—that while Nature seems to promise a perfect way, we had better not try to grasp it. Though the laws of men and their best rules of conduct sometimes work cruel injustice, they are not as utterly devastating as are man's puny efforts to understand the absolute laws of infinity, if there be any. Captain Vere said:

> 'Well, I, too, feel the full force of that [the higher law]. It is Nature. But do these buttons we wear attest that our allegiance is to Nature? No, to the King. Though the ocean, which is inviolate Nature primeval, though this be the element where we move and have our being as sailors, yet as the King's officers lies our duty in a sphere correspondingly natural? . . . Our vowed responsibility is this: That however pitilessly that law [martial law] may operate, we nevertheless adhere to it and administer it.'

But Melville does more in *Billy Budd* than underscore a conclusion long since foreshadowed in his earlier novels. This last book discloses, also, his unhappy reasons for accepting the position he had so long protested. If he had been able, he would have plumbed the depths of truth, identified himself with it, and would have found the peace he sought. Alternatively, he would have welcomed the knowledge that final truth is irrelevant to man's life, and would have sought some penultimate, man-created framework that would efficiently ignore ultimate understandings. But neither option described for Melville the actuality in which a man spends his days. Truth could not be captured, and it could not be ignored. He uses John Claggart, in *Billy Budd,* to dramatize his concept of man that prevented him from crowning the efforts of Taji, Ahab, or Pierre with success, that defeated the possibility of Budd's innocence, and that caused Ishmael and Captain Vere to be afflicted with a cosmic melancholy.

Claggart, the master-at-arms aboard the *Indomitable,* is the victim of Billy Budd's outraged and convulsive blow. He is the one, who, for no necessary reason, falsely accuses Billy to Captain Vere; and he is the man for whose murder Billy Budd has to hang. He is the instrument by whom Budd's innocence matures in a shocking second to experience of good and evil. It is through him that Melville tells us why man must suffer the ills he suffers, and why he may harbor reasonably no wishful dream of content in his life as a man.

The master-at-arms comprehends far more than Billy Budd of the human nature that he and Billy share, of course; it is possible that he possesses a deeper knowledge of man than does Captain Vere, though the disciplined character of the Captain may conceal an equal comprehension. Claggart was one of the "true madmen," one who had "willed malice" and "had experienced the reactionary bite of that serpent." He had, said Melville, "no power to annul the elemental evil in himself," and he therefore hated with a burning passion the young sailor who was yet innocent, and who had not lost his chance to perceive the good and become it. Completely depraved, John Claggart did not have to have a reason to attack Billy Budd; the Handsome Sailor was loathsome to him just because he existed. So it was that the master-at-arms carefully planned Billy's destruction. Captain Vere was powerless to hinder the tragedy; he could only be the more tormented as he understood it better.

It might still be argued that Billy Budd was an unlucky innocent, who might have chanced not to meet his Claggart. But Melville will have none of this interpretation. He points out, before Claggart is introduced into the narrative, that Billy Budd, for all his shining beauty and unblemished character, did have a defect, a stutter that could become even more than a stutter under the proper stress. He commented on this flaw:

> In this particular Billy was a striking instance that the arch interpreter, the envious marplot of Eden, still has more or less to do with every human consignment to this planet of earth.

Billy Budd's innocence cannot be preserved because he is not innocent. He is unawakened to the potential of evil

within him, but he is not without it. Poor Billy was not merely unfortunate in his meeting with John Claggart, he was
fated to meet him somewhere, sometime. That his meeting
came on a warship was accidental; that the names of the
characters were what they were was also accidental. But that
innocence becomes knowledge of good and evil was not an
accident.

Melville's last search for meaning failed, as had the others.
There was nothing for him to do but approve Captain Vere's
agonized expediency. Even that approval he could not give
without qualification, for Captain Vere is wounded to death
in a sea battle with the *Atheiste,* and dies murmuring the
name of Billy Budd. There was no personal victory for Vere,
or for Melville, in reluctant acceptance of the attainable.

When done, Melville put his book into a pigeon hole in
his roll-top desk, to be found or not, as the "heartless voids"
might dictate.

STETSON UNIVERSITY

- *A Danforth, Woodrow Wilson, and Rotary Fellow,* DA-VID MARCELL *has studied at Stetson University, St. Andrews in Scotland, and Yale. His doctoral dissertation in American Studies is concerned with changing American attitudes toward the idea of progress.*

High Ideals and Catchpenny Realities in Henry James's "The Portrait of a Lady"

HENRY JAMES'S PSYCHOLOGICAL MASTERPIECE, *The Portrait of a Lady,* is a study of an unfolding ideal and a growing consciousness. It is the highly integrated tracing of a young woman "in motion"—of a noble spirit "affronting" its destiny and emerging chastened but not completely vanquished. (Preface to the New York Edition) Indeed, Isabel Archer, though the victim of an "unimaginable" deceit and her own "beastly" innocence, has at the end a painful triumph: she finds the courage to reject an unworthy ideal and accept a dolorous fate in the service of a higher calling.

From all outward appearances Isabel's history is unremarkable. An orphan, captured (not "adopted") by a wealthy aunt and brought to England from Albany, she is one of the leaders of James's long parade of "innocents abroad." Her uncle dies and leaves her a fortune. Inexperienced and romantic, the girl is led into marriage, and after three years finds her lofty aspirations brought hopelessly down, her marriage a miserable encumbrance, and her husband harboring a malevolent hatred for her. She learns that her dearest friend is in truth the mother of her step-

child and the engineer of her marriage—a marriage calcu-
lated to provide the child with a dowry of her own. Faced
with the alternative of flight and disavowal, Isabel accepts
the responsibility for her choice of marriage and thus, as
Quenten Anderson has put it, she "steps into the adult
world"—a sadder but much, much wiser girl.

Isabel's initiation would be prosaic enough if James were
less brilliant a craftsman and observer of the human spirit. By artfully placing the center of action in the girl's
own mind, however, he shows in intriguing fashion "what
an exciting inward life may do for the person leading it
even while it remains perfectly normal." It is Isabel's "sense"
for her adventures which make them "the stuff of . . .
'story'." (Preface) The suspense mounts with her growing
awareness of her hostile ambiance—an awareness in which
James discreetly allows the reader to share. The reader's
own responses are an integral part of the drama.

Isabel's ideal — what she comes to call "the aristocratic
situation"—is not presented as a *fait accompli*. Rather, in
the first half of the book we are permitted to see her vision
grow naturally out of her "envelope of circumstances." As
she matures, her perception becomes more acute, and her
ideal becomes more conscious and refined; finally, on the
strength of that ideal she marries Gilbert Osmond. Her decision to marry puts her ideal to the brutal test of what
James regards as the real world: the world of whirling social
forces and awareness. The last half of *The Portrait* depicts
the crushing impingement of that world upon her ideal and
the heroic response Isabel makes despite her shattered illusions.

When Mrs. Touchett first discovers her, Isabel is seated
in the "mysterious apartment" next to the library in her
grandmother's house, and she is "trudging over the sandy
plains of a history of German Thought." In this room the
girl has provided her own education; as a child, after only
one day in the schoolhouse across the street, she had protested against its laws and been allowed to stay at home to

lay her own foundation of knowledge. She has had "uncontrolled use" of the library of books; her selection, we are told, has been guided chiefly by the appeal of the frontispiece —a criterion which nevertheless allows her to consume a history of philosophical idealism.

The room in which she reads is sealed off from the street by a bolted door whose sidelights have been covered over with green paper. The girl theorizes that there is a "strange, unseen place on the other side—a place which became to the child's imagination, according to its different moods, a region of delight or of terror." From this room she used to hear the hum of childish voices from the school across the street—"an incident in which the elation of liberty and the pain of exclusion were indistinguishably mingled."

In this one short scene Isabel is shown to be intelligent and enterprising, as well as rebellious and independent. Her intuition and imagination are brought out vividly, as is her exclusiveness and sense of superiority. The room is a nursery where the girl's native properties and inclinations have flourished unrestricted. She has become reliant on her own resources to furnish her own amusement, although, most significantly, her adventures have all been vicarious; her most valuable experiences have come from her reading. In a sense, the entire novel can be seen as the crashing down of the walls of this natal room.

At Gardencourt Isabel's ideal evolves and takes form. Even before she arrives in England, we know that she is "a young woman of many theories," but at the Touchett's stately home—after exposure to the climate of an older, more complex civilization—we see these theories cohere in an overarching metaphor.

During the first few days with the Touchetts Isabel seems the typical irreverent American tourist. She speaks crudely about "specimens" of English life and inquires skeptically, if half humorously, about the family ghost. In the weeks following, however, her social development is rapid; she no longer regards her companions as on display solely for her amusement. Her progress—her "motion"—can be seen best when contrasted with the stability of such flat characters as Mrs. Touchett and Henrietta Stackpole. (See Richard Poirier, *The Comic Sense of Henry James.)*

Isabel's ideas—and she has a multitude of them—are not so much the product of firm convictions as they are reactions to provocation. If her responses at times seem inconsistent, it is because she does not respond according to what she feels, but rather to what she thinks she ought to feel. Her conception of the kind of person she thinks she would like to be is romantic in the extreme, and it zooms with her fancy; her decisions are primarily functions of a somewhat capricious self-image.

Her pride—her desire to "think well of herself"—is her most remarkable feature. Isabel wishes to be free to choose her fate, to fly in the face of the gods of necessity. When she refuses the almost too perfect Lord Warburton's proposal she says, "I can't escape my fate. . . . I should try to escape it if I were to marry you." In reality, his offer simply fails to stimulate her imagination. Her refusal is based on primarily negative considerations: "the idea failed to support any enlightened prejudice in favor of the free exploration of life she had hitherto entertained or was now capable of entertaining." Isabel is not sure at this stage what her ideal actually is, but she is rather certain what it is not.

Gradually her ideal matures and becomes a little more positive. From a general desire to remain free from any obligation "to take a restricted view," Isabel comes specifically to value the advantages deriving from a superior perception. When she realizes that Madame Merle's broad experience would enable her to encompass the rather two-dimensional Henrietta while Henrietta would only partially understand Madame Merle, she surmises:

'That's the great thing . . .; that's the supreme good fortune: to be able to be in a better position for appreciating people than they are for appreciating you. And she added that such, when one considered it, was simply the essence of the aristo-

cratic situation. In this light, if in no other, one should aim
at the aristocratic situation.

This, then, embellished and applied, becomes her ideal:
to be in a position to see, to know, to perceive without being held accountable for that knowledge and those perceptions—always to be able to escape from the obligations of
the knowledge she acquires. Moreover, she desires knowledge without the attending pain and involvement of the
learning process. When Ralph comments, "You want to
drain the cup of experience," she replies accurately: "No, I
don't wish to touch the cup of experience. It's poisoned
drink! I only want to see for myself." Ralph, with equal
accuracy, observes, "You want to see, but not to feel." Isabel
wants to view the world in its entirety without having to
respond to what she observes.

The imagery of Isabel's concept of herself and the "aristocratic situation" is predominantly spatial; it shows graph-
ically the exclusiveness of her ideal and her preoccupation
with freedom. "High places of happiness," the "independent
class," "lengthening vistas"—all show the self-sufficiency of
her imagined qualities and aspirations. She regards any attempt to obligate herself as a "trap"; Lord Warburton's "system" would for her be but a "vast cage" limiting her possibilities and her free-wheeling imagination. Similarly, Ralph
thinks of her "sailing in the bright lights, over the heads of
men."

With fine insight and control, James shows how his
heroine's point of view develops; further, he shows how this
point of view fatally excludes the possibility of her seeing
other points of view. The exquisite irresponsibility of the
"aristocratic situation" precludes the engagement necessary
for effective social exchange. *The desire to be limitless becomes in itself a limitation.* In presenting her developing
ideal, James is careful not to push her cause too vigorously.
Criticism of her ideas comes from both Ralph and Madame
Merle, who serve to point up the ironic narrowness of her
thinking.

In the famous "metaphysical discussion" between Isabel and Madame Merle the area of disagreement is fundamental, and Madame Merle wisely ends their talk abruptly. Before she does so, however, the opposing points of view are starkly juxtaposed, and Isabel's pride and vulnerability stand revealed. Significantly, the discussion begins over the question of marrying for practical advantage and turns on the definition of the "self." Isabel's notion of "success"—a rather hazy desire to see some dream of youth come true—commences the discussion. Inevitably, the talk turns to "the young man with the moustache" and how one judges him. Madame Merle's position, that one must be judged by one's choices —by one's "things," by "one's expression of one's self," by "some cluster of appurtenances"—is offensive to Isabel's idealism. In contrast, she maintains that nothing except herself is expressive of her self. "Nothing that belongs to me is any measure of me; everything's on the contrary a limit, a barrier, and a perfectly arbitrary one." The upshot of the talk is that Isabel is shown to have no adequate definition of the "self" with which to regard and evaluate other selves —a deficiency which proves catastrophic when she meets Gilbert Osmond.

Although Madame Merle provides a sharp contrast to Isabel's innocence, her main function is that of the betrayer. Unfortunately, James's delineation of her as the Judas-figure is rather uncharacteristically clumsy, but there is no missing the point. If Madame Merle is the betrayer, however—if she did engineer her friend's marriage to her former lover and the father of her child—she certainly did not force the girl into anything. Madame Merle's betrayal is more a sin of omission than of commission: she simply does not reveal the full history of her relationship to Osmond. Why, then, if no one coerces her, does Isabel fall for the "sterile dilettante," the only character in the book with absolutely no redeeming qualities? The answer, of course, lies in Isabel's own imagination.

Osmond succeeds where other, worthier men have failed

primarily because he is a part of no discernable "system." Both Caspar Goodwood and Lord Warburton—the latter particularly—operate in a prescribed social circuit in which their lives and the alternatives they will be able to consider are easily conceived. Not so with Osmond. He is a man of no "attachments," of no past, and with no easily foreseeable future. When he first meets Isabel he is quite candid in relating his sketchy circumstances; her imagination, however, James tells us, "supplied the human element which she was sure had not been wanting." What she cannot see in Osmond she imagines, and thus he becomes the hero of her romance.

Had Osmond been a more positive figure—again, like Caspar Goodwood or Lord Warburton—he would have done violence to Isabel's imaginings and thus not have been a suitable candidate for her idealization. His life, as he informs her, has been deliberately negative; or, as he allows in answer to her questioning, "call it affirmative if you like. Only it has affirmed my indifference. Mind you, not my natural indifference—I *had* none. But my studied, wilful renunciation." Osmond appears to defer to no one in making his decisions; he renounces all obligations except the demands of good taste, and he himself defines what that good taste shall be. As he tells Isabel, "I'm convention itself." This conscious rejection of external pressures in favor of a life given solely to the gratification of esthetic sensibilities appeals strongly to the young heiress, and—inevitably, it would seem—she comes to believe that only with Osmond will she be able to attain the "aristocratic situation."

James felt the most important and effective part of the book was Isabel's fireside epiphany wherein for the first time she allows herself to assess realistically what her marriage has become, and, even more importantly, to recognize the fact that she herself has been at least partially responsible for her own unhappiness. The revelation comes as a *donné* —as the perception of an all-important insight occasioned by a minute detail which makes a complex experience understandable. Her observation of the intimacy of Madame Merle and Osmond—an intimacy she no longer shares with either—causes her to realize fully the threat her many ideas and aspirations have posed to her insecure, hypocritical husband, and her own part in the development of his hatred for her. She sees, ironically, in the light of the "metaphysical discussion," that it was precisely Osmond's carefully chosen "cluster of appurtenances" which she had misinterpreted. He who seemed so indifferent to the outside world was actually the least indifferent of all her associates; he was the last person in the world with whom she could have realized her ideal. Moreover, like the good connoisseur he professed to be, he had "collected" both her and her money. Osmond's acute awareness of and painful sensitivity to the opinions of others has become the very cage she sought to escape. Although Ralph had perceived her suitor's subtle posturing before her marriage, his warnings had been to no avail.

Despite her perception, Isabel's innocence still prevents her from guessing what a more experienced person would have known. As the Countess Gemini exclaims before revealing that Madame Merle is really Pansy's mother, "You never suspected because you've got such a beastly pure mind." On learning the full depravity of the trap in which she has been snared, Isabel realizes with horror the effect of her conceited innocence on Ralph. R. W. B. Lewis in *The American Adam* comments that James recognized "that the condition prior to conscience might have insidious undertones of the amoral as well as the beguiling naiveté of the premoral." This is exactly the sophisticated perception Isabel is finally able to make: that self-absorbed innocence can be cruel as well as vulnerable. Her return to Gardencourt is in search of forgiveness and atonement for the blindness of her ideal.

The novel ends rather abruptly. Isabel, we know, has achieved the tragic view; she has seen the ghost at Gardencourt. In going back to Rome and her marriage she nevertheless leaves several issues unresolved, and many critics dissatisfied. James realized that the novel's *denouement* was inconclusive and that this would be regarded by some as a weakness; he anticipated their criticism in his notebook:

> The whole of anything is never told; you can only take what hangs together. What I have done has that unity—it groups together. It is not complete in itself—and the rest may be taken up or not, later.

Despite the criticism of the ending there is an admirable symmetry to the *Portrait*. Isabel's sin is the sin of pride; her penance is apposite. She assumed that she could choose the nature of her experience and hence determine her fate. Her denial notwithstanding, she did "want to see, but not to feel." She assumed also that she could exist as a thing apart and still enjoy full knowledge of the world and its possibilities. Her assumptions did not take into account the fact that she, like other mortals, was the product of her total experience, and that her understanding and perceptions were conditioned by the variety and richness of that experience. By deliberately attempting to prohibit herself from any kind of total involvement, she unwittingly restricted the limits of her knowledge — in her mind, as James informs us, "The love of knowledge coexisted with the finest capacity for ignorance" — so that when she finally did commit herself completely her decision was based on naive appraisal of the man she married.

"Experience," James wrote in *The Princess Cassimassima,* "is the apprehension of ourselves as social beings." This is the knowledge Isabel has gained as she returns to Rome to confront her fate. Hitherto she strove to isolate herself from obligations which she feared would be cloying; by returning to Italy she accepts—for life, perhaps—the burden of Pansy's love and dependency, and the bond of a hate-filled marriage. She acknowledges willingly her accountability for her decision; her innocent ideal of freedom has given way to a compassionate recognition of duty and responsibility. Although her future is to be cruelly fettered, by accepting her fate she becomes a lady of heroic proportions.

YALE UNIVERSITY

• *SY KAHN received his degrees from the University of Pennsylvania, the University of Connecticut, and the University of Wisconsin. He has taught at Beloit College, held a Fulbright lectureship in Greece, and teaches now at the University of South Florida.*

Stephen Crane and the Giant Voice in the Night: An Explication of "The Monster"

ONE OF THE MOST UNUSUAL, attractive literary careers among American writers is that of Stephen Crane. The last ten years of literary scholarship have not only rescued that career but not only rescued that career but also intensively examined it. Crane's life and work invite every sort of literary criticism. The paradoxes, ironies, flamboyancies of his personal life prompt psychoanalytical speculations; the highly patterned prose is honey to the busy bees of the new criticism, and the imagistic, spare, ironic poetry that anticipates the Imagists of the 20th century, the themes and situations that foreshadow Ernest Hemingway and the expatriates, delight the literary historian. It might take a dark, slender, ironic Crane to appreciate fully the critical consequences of his life and work. Time and scholarship have given him a currency and respectability he did not always enjoy in his own brief life.

Crane has been "discovered" several times during this century, in the periods following both world wars. It is natural that the post-war atmosphere should be propitious for an interest in Crane's work. Then there is time to evaluate the experience of war and the ambiguous events through which we have passed and survived. He speaks to us with the special accents of the sensitive veteran who has known physical or psychological wounding and whose ironic, under-stated tone often masks his compassion.

The fact that Crane wrote *The Red Badge of Courage* before he actually experienced war alerts us to his angle of vision. From the beginning of his career he saw men "at war." His Bowery tales, his Western stories, his famous "The Open Boat" are as much about wounded, pressured men as are his war tales. He was by temperament a naturalist who saw man as a creature at the center of enormous, monstrous forces and fighting for survival against heavy odds. Survival with integrity made the odds even longer. It is the micro-cosm of war that frequently provides Crane with an arena for his drama. War is his richest symbol for man's condition; it dramatizes and intensifies his usual dilemmas.

Crane artistically rendered the raw experiences of war in a special, prismatic prose, in color-shot imagery and elegant impressions. It is a world where each sound is amplified by human terror, each color made brilliant and blaring by the frightened, wary eye, and the enemy invested with one's deepest, primitive fears. All this Crane instinctively knew in *The Red Badge of Courage.* In the fictional world of war, Crane's ironic vision, his talent for bizarre imagery, his curious religious and biblical diction (by which he inflates the egoistic actions and poses of his characters for later puncturing by pointed, ironic understatement) , and his im-pressionistic descriptions could find their most ample ex-pression. Crane's young soldier, Henry Fleming, like Hem-ingway's Nick Adams, finds himself thrust into a world that shocks him into new levels of feeling and perception; the two men are symbols of innocence blasted by violence, by what at worst seems an intelligent malevolence.

Both Crane and Hemingway began with a sense of irony, a gift for understatement, an abhorrence of sentimentalism and a view of man that made war one of the important, inevitable metaphors for dramatizing their insights. Man under stress, at the center of powerful, irrational forces, man forging and tempering an answerable courage and code is the repetitive situation at the center of both writers' works. They both assert that in heaven there is *nada,* that nature is indifferent, that the uninitiated, unwounded are ignorantly cruel and barbarously sentimental. Only the scarred can hope to offer even a tentative interpretation of man's dilemmas.

In the novelette *The Monster,* one of his most effective works, Crane again projects his central situation of man under attack by irrational forces. By employing many of the devices of his war fiction, especially patterns of sound and fire images which symbolize threatening, evil human forces, he evokes a war-like world in which sound and color are amplified and intensified. Dr. Trescott finds himself at war with the townspeople because he chooses to maintain Henry Johnson, his Negro stableman, in the town rather than commit him to an institution. Johnson risked his life saving young Jimmie Trescott, the doctor's son, from a fire in Trescott's house. However, while carrying the terrified Jimmie through the blazing laboratory, Johnson is overcome. The boy is saved by his father. Johnson, lying face up under a spilled chemical, has his face burned away. Under the doctor's care he survives this disfigurement, but the injury renders him mindless as well as faceless. Thus he becomes a shambling, mumbling "monster" who innocently, harmlessly terrorizes the town. The irony is quickly apparent; the more the townspeople irrationally react to Johnson, the more monstrous they appear. Johnson is a monster in appearance only; the townspeople, because of their terror and eventual persecution of Dr. Trescott, are monstrous in essence.

The Monster is an especially fruitful story for an understanding of Crane. Written fairly late in his short career, in England during 1897 following his return from the Greco-Turkish War, it brings into focus not only a number of Crane's themes and attitudes but also permits him to dramatize personal piques and tensions. By the time Crane arrived in England in 1897, with Cora Taylor, his unofficial wife, on his arm, he had known enough of life, war, fame and society to have brought his ironic observations and wit to a fine edge. Numerous events in his life reveal that he frequently contested the judgments and conventions of his society. He had escorted small boys to barber shops to have their Little Lord Fauntleroy hair styles shorn, much to the outrage of mothers. He had made newspaper headlines defending prostitutes from the New York police. He had been attacked in the press, rumored to be a profligate and dope addict. His prose and poetry had encountered outraged, hostile criticism; fellow writers reviewed his work with ridicule, prompted perhaps by misunderstanding or jealousy. That various wounds were lively in him is revealed in a letter he wrote to his brother, William Crane, in October, 1897, not long after he had completed *The Monster*. "There seem so many of them in America who want to kill, bury and forget me purely out of unkindness and envy and—my unworthiness, if you choose."

Now he was in England with Cora, she not yet divorced from her second husband, and both of them subject to gossip and sometimes subterfuge to mask their illegal relationship. Furthermore, he had written novels and stories about an American soldier who ran away from a battle (though later a hero), about a girl driven to prostitution and suicide, about Bowery derelicts impelled by ruthless social forces rather than flaws of character. To those more inclined to gossip than to intelligent reading, the works merely supported erroneous notions about Crane's character. He was always at war with the misjudging mob, with philistines and with ruthless conventions. His expatriation and death abroad give testimony to the hostility he felt, and much of his work, and particularly *The Monster*, project the tensions between himself and society.

The Monster excoriates the citizens of Whilomville, the once-upon-a-time town, the Port Jervis of Crane's youth. Crane had some scores to settle, some wounds to salve, some ghosts to exorcise. Early and throughout the story Crane points up the conventionality and misjudgments of the townspeople which set them at a distance from the truth. As Henry Johnson, gorgeously arrayed after his day's work, struts through town to visit Bella Farragut of Watermelon Lane, he passes a group of lounging young men who discuss "everything with critical insight, passing the whole town in review as it swarmed in the street." Crane reinforces the scorn he feels for easy judgments when a moment later he has the older men in Reifsnyder's barber shop watch Henry and others pass before the plate-glass window as they might fish in an aquarium. They argue whether this is Henry or not; they are confused by his finery as later they are to be terrorized by his facelessness. Both reactions to the Negro are based on appearances. The townspeople, like the gossiping, strolling groups of girls Crane describes, give evidence to a "curious public dependence upon one another which was their inheritance."

The town's gift for hasty misjudgment is more sharply dramatized at the scene of the fire. Spectators erroneously assume that Henry and Jimmie are dead, that Henry overturned a lamp while sitting up with a sick Jimmie; and another man, "always preserved for the deliverance of the final judgment," said, " 'Oh, they'll die sure. Burned to flinders. No chance. Hull lot of them.' " The morning newspaper announces Johnson's death. While rumors rage, "flags of fire . . . waved joyfully against the black sky. The bells of the town were clashing unceasingly." Conflagration and cacaphony symbolize the heat and noise of the townspeople all through the work. In typical patterning, Crane makes many references to harsh sounds in the town which amplify the gossip and rumors of the people and foreshadow their angry voices. When Crane tells us early in the story about the young men of "critical insight," he also calls attention to the gongs of the electric cars. The fire engines "clang," the bells "peal," swinging "the heart to and fro, up and down, with each peal of it," as the town rushes to the fire. Finally there is a "brazen din" as all the churches and school-houses send out the alarm. "There was also a kind of rivalry as to which bell should be made to produce the greatest din." A "sinister" factory whistle announces the fire like "a giant voice in the night." It is this voice made human that shouts down reason and compassion in Whilomville. The attention to sounds, fire and color in insistent, repetitive patterns of imagery distinctly recall the war world of Henry Fleming (another Henry caught in a conflagration). It is war again for Crane, a monstrous world of roar and fire, only this time the enemy is the townspeople, at first merely conforming and misjudging, but later fearful, outraged and, finally, vicious.

Henry, contrary to rumor, survives, and Whilomville's children who once chanted, "Nigger, nigger, never die. Black face and shiny eye," are silenced. Meanwhile the demented Henry, attended in Judge Hagenthorpe's house by Dr. Trescott, has his faceless head swathed in bandages except for one unwinking eye that, like Dr. Eckleburg's eyes in *The Great Gatsby*, stares at the moral wasteland. Immediately there is doubt as to the "questionable charity in preserving this negro's life," that it was a "blunder of virtue," and later there is the implication that a dead Henry will avoid trouble and embarrassment to the town. That it is a matter of conscience for Dr. Trescott to save and to care for Henry carries less weight for the people than their fears of a harmless, helpless Negro. Thus Crane reveals the moral facelessness of Whilomville, unmasking it with the red acid of his prose.

When Johnson is sufficiently recovered, he is boarded at the home of Alek Williams. One evening Johnson shambles away into town, first frightening little Sadie Winter at a children's party as he ambles toward Watermelon Alley. He reduces the Farragut family to terror and flight as the blithe Henry idiotically, reiteratively requests of Bella " 'the magnifercent gratitude of you' company' " to a dance. Meanwhile the "magnifercent company" shudders face down and wailing on the floor, the obese Mrs. Farragut scales a high fence and Young Sim, with soundless terror, falls backwards off the porch railing. Later the Police Chief reports to Trescott that

following the Watermelon Alley fiasco, Johnson, in his quest
for company, " 'stampeded the whole outfit,' " that an old
woman broke her leg getting over a fence, that on Main
Street an Irish girl threw a fit, and " 'there was sort of a
riot.' " Henry ends up running, stoned by a large crowd; he
finishes the evening in jail under the protection of the Police
Chief.

Crane further dramatizes his castigation of Whilomville
in a scene between Dr. Trescott and Jake Winter, father of
the frightened, now ill, Sadie. At Winter's house, where he
goes to administer to the girl because the family doctor is
out of town, he is roughly greeted by an irate father. Then
Trescott realizes that "he had heard an utterly new challenge
in the night of the jungle." His solicitude and prescription
for the little girl evoke Winter's "fiery rage"; he "barks" at
the doctor, "yelping" at him from the front porch. Much
earlier in the story, before the fire, Crane tells us that Trescott in successfully treating a case felt that the malady "was
now in complete obedience to him, like a wild animal that
he had subdued." It becomes clear that Trescott has no prescription for the new ailments of the town which have turned once friendly voices into angry, animal retorts. The "fiery
rage" mounts, and just as "the fire-imps calling and calling,
clan joining clan" had earlier destroyed the doctor's house,
the people, inflamed by outrage and terror, clannishly gather
to destroy the doctor.

That Crane had old animosities to resolve is everywhere
apparent in the tale. In the character Martha Goodwin he
took the opportunity to air a three year old hostility. A
letter written in 1894 from Port Jervis describes the prototype of Martha.

> There is a feminine mule up here who has aroused all the
> bloodthirst in me and I don't know where it will end. She
> has no more brains than a pig and all she does is sit in her
> kitchen and grunt. But when she grunts something dies howl-
> ing. It may be a girl's reputation or a political party or the
> Baptist Church but it stops in its tracks and dies. Sunday I

took a 13 year old child out driving in a buggy. Monday this
mule addresses me in front of the barber's and says, 'You was
drivin[g] Frances out yesterday' and grunted. At once all present knew that Frances and I should be hanged on twin gallows
for red sins. No man is strong enough to attack this mummy
because she is a nice woman. She looks like a dried bean and
has no sense, but she is a nice woman. . . . Now, my friend,
there is a great joke in all this. This lady in her righteousness is just the grave of a stale lust and every boy in town
knows it. She accepted ruin at the hands of a farmer when
we were all 10 or 11. But she is a nice woman and all her
views of all things belong on the table of Moses.

Martha is single, lives with a married sister in Whilomville. She has "adamantine opinions" about the people in
the town and the world in general, from the situation in
Armenia to the latest local flirtation. For all dilemmas she
advocates drastic measures. "For instance she contended
that all Turks should be pushed into the sea and drowned,
and that Mrs. Minster and young Griscom should be hanged
side by side on twin gallows." Martha's fire and vindictive-
ness, like her prototype's, spring from disappointment in
love, and now, "In regard to social misdemeanors, she who
was simply the mausoleum of a dead passion was probably
the most savage critic in town."

The first judgment rendered by this formidable woman
upon hearing the news of Johnson's stroll through the town
is that it would serve Trescott right if he lost all his patients.
Later in the story, however, it is she, curiously, who becomes
the voice of reason. The local ladies tell Martha about
Winter's anger and that Sadie Winter has been ill ever since
Johnson got loose. Martha is quick to correct them; she has
seen Sadie going to school since that time. Suddenly she
switches her alliance to Trescott against Winter. When the
ladies argue that she " 'can't go against the whole town,' "
Martha retorts, " 'Do you call those silly people who are
scared of Henry Johnson "the whole town"?' " These ladies
who have not seen Johnson are terrified by him because

"everybody says" he is monstrous. Martha bedevils them further, questioning why they are frightened about what they have not seen, and then humanely remarks that even if she were scared by Johnson's appearance, she would " 'try not to be afraid of him.' "

How, then, are we to reconcile the apparently conflicting pictures of Martha as an opinionated, ferocious gossip and at the same time one of the few rational minds in the aroused town? Certainly in this last appearance she seems to speak for Crane, a rational voice among the hysterical harridans. Even her name, Goodwin, suggests she is the breadth of reason, but ultimately she is the "good wind" that blows no good. She is essentially tendentious, vindictive and perversely combative; her pleasure is not in justice but in defeating her cronies. Thus in Crane's quixotic world she is accurate about Sadie and seemingly humane and compassionate toward Trescott and Johnson, not because she is thoughtful, kind and generous, but rather out of a negative, bitter and perverse nature that compensates for her frustrations. Crane's irony extends even to the woman who speaks most sympathetically about Henry. His revenge for old wounds is subtle, exquisite and complete.

Crane employs another important device for scoring Whilomville. He frequently focuses our attention upon the children who are, like their parents, full of superstitions, rumors and misinformation. Late in the story Jimmie and his friends, playing near the veiled, isolated, hymn-singing Johnson, urge each other to touch the faceless stableman. Finally Jimmie and another small hero manage this bravery. However, the terror of the boys parallels the hysteria of their elders. Among the children these irrationalities are understandable, forgiveable, but when Crane has both children and most adults reacting similarly, almost all the adults of Whilomville stand condemned.

Near the end of *The Monster* a delegation of Whilomville's leading citizens pay a call on Trescott to urge him to give up care of Henry. John Twelve, reported to be worth over a million, but actually worth only $400,000, Crane writes, keeping up the pattern of distortion of fact in Whilomville, warns Trescott that he has fallen from being the leading doctor in town to the last. Trescott, however, remains adamant in his stand on Johnson. He will keep him in town and care for him.

The final section of the story provides us with a tableau symbolizing the ostracism and isolation which not only Trescott but his family must suffer because of his decision. He arrives home on a Wednesday evening, recalling that Wednesday is the day his wife "receives." He finds her crying and complaining of a headache. It appears that only Mrs. Twelve stopped by. There are fifteen unused teacups to testify to the town's response to his integrity. As the Doctor comforts his wife, the whining wind and slanting snow emphasize their isolation, and "the coal in the stove settled with a crumbling sound, and the four panes of mica flashed a sudden new crimson." These last, subdued images of sound and fire, the flare and mutter, understate, obliquely comment on the weariness of the scene. The conflagration is over.

In *The Monster* Crane achieves a beautiful integration of themes and devices characteristic of his total work. Sound, light and animal images, similar to those used in the war fiction, particularly *The Red Badge of Courage*, evoke a total image of man at war with giant forces. Most surely the fire that destroyed the Trescott home and rendered Johnson faceless, described as "alive with envy, hatred and malice," is the symbol of the conflagration of feelings that scorch Trescott in his battle of conscience. In depicting scene after scene of Whilomville's gossip-mongering stupidity, its misbegotten judgments and baseless fears, Crane was able through the ritual of the story to work out many sharply felt antagonisms and to bring balm to old wounds. Trescott's ostracism and Johnson's isolation are creations that spring from Crane's own sense of rejection by his countrymen because of his own intense fidelity to literary themes and principles, his reaction to social injustices sometimes ridiculed and attacked as blunders of virtue. Here was "a story with some sense in it" he explosively explained after Richard Watson Gilder of the *Century* had rejected it and Crane's friend Harold Frederick had advised him to discard it. The "sense" and sensibility that Crane often demonstrated in his work had often been misread and misunderstood. Irony, often imperfectly grasped by his readers, then as now, is crucial to his work.

The Monster was printed in *Harper's Weekly* in August, 1898, about a year after its completion. Like Henry Johnson, the story had suffered rejection because of its surface horror. It stands, however, as an answer to that sinister "giant voice in the night," that "challenge in the night of the jungle" which are the savage voices of Whilomville. Crane had, as the Chief of Police says of Johnson, " 'been hurt up to the limit.' " Less than two years after the publication of *The Monster* Crane was dead in Germany. The story remains one of his most effective expressions of and responses to the voices he heard and the wounds he felt.

UNIVERSITY OF SOUTH FLORIDA

• GUY OWEN received his PhD at the University of North Carolina, has taught at Stetson University for six years, and will be teaching at North Carolina State University in the fall of 1962. He is a widely published poet and short story writer, and his first novel — SEASON OF FEAR—was published by Random House in 1960.

Imagery and

Meaning in

"The Great Gatsby"

IN SPITE OF MY QUALIFIED admiration for *The Great Gatsby* I am one of those who stubbornly remain skeptical about the current Fitzgerald revival, insisting that his reputation is now overblown, due largely to the fascination of his legendary and symbolic life and the present intense interest in the ideas and literature of the 1920's. That Fitzgerald is now widely read there is no denying. Almost all his work is back in print, along with ephemeral pieces that should have remained in limbo. No doubt much of this interest will be shortlived, since a good deal of it is based on nothing more substantial than Bud Shulberg's *The Disenchanted,* Sheila Graham's *Beloved Infidel,* and Mr. Gregory Peck. In the long run, I suspect that a writer's reputation cannot be entrusted to either Hollywood script writers or his surviving mistresses.

Not that I wish to deny Fitzgerald talent, even genius. I simply maintain that he dissipated his very large gifts and failed to realize his potentialities except in *The Great Gatsby, Tender is the Night,* a few scenes in *The Last Tycoon,* and a handful of short stories. To be sure, this is a great deal, but it is not enough for a lifetime devoted to writing; for even Fitzgerald's best novels contain very serious weaknesses. Fitzgerald stated the case well when he called himself "a first-rate writer who has never produced anything but second-rate books." Reading Arthur Mizener's excellent biography, *The Far Side of Paradise,* and Fitzgerald's own *The Crack-up* leaves one with a sense of tragic waste.

Yet notwithstanding my misgivings about Fitzgerald as an artist, I find that I keep returning to *The Great Gatsby,* which is generally acknowledged to be Fitzgerald's masterpiece. However, I share Maxwell Geismar's uneasiness about *Gatsby* and I am reluctant to label it a "classic"—whatever that means—as do most critics. Though *The Great Gatsby* is a seriously flawed novel, I find it almost continuously interesting—and not for the usual reasons.

I do not, for example, agree that *Gatsby* is great because it successfully mirrors its age; in fact the novel is much too thin to accomplish all that. The larger canvases of Wolfe and Lewis are better suited to rendering an age. Nor do I find in it any unusual depth of characterization. To be truthful, Fitzgerald is barely competent in the development of his characters in *Gatsby.* The novelist agreed in part with H. L. Mencken, who said that Fitzgerald had failed to get "under the skin of its people." Daisy Buchanan comes alive only as a voice—though of course Fitzgerald wanted her to seem unreal in one sense. More damaging, Gatsby himself is not adequately probed. As both Edith Wharton and Maxwell Perkins wrote Fitzgerald, Gatsby remains too mysterious, and I feel that at times his actions are insufficiently motivated. It is difficult to "see" Gatsby, to identify with him as a total being. Fitzgerald wrote in a letter to John Peale Bishop,

> Also you are right about Gatsby being blurred and patchy. I never at any one time saw him clear myself—for he started out as one man I knew and then changed into myself—the amalgam was never complete in my mind.

Moreover, Nick Carroway, the narrator, lacks genuine warmth, and other characters—Wolfsheim, for instance—remain static caricatures.

Nor is the plot, although it is beautifully balanced and controlled, rich enough to reward close scrutiny. Mencker, once again, referred to it as "no more than a glorified anecdote." Certainly it must be admitted that the switching of the cars at the crucial moment and Daisy's killing her rival Myrtle Wilson seem rather fortuitous.

Finally, Fitzgerald's handling of the point of view is hopelessly inept at times. He was still struggling with the problems of the angle of vision—and still trying to learn from Joseph Conrad—in *The Last Tycoon*.

If this much can be asserted by way of indictment of *Gatsby*, what then holds the novel together and makes it for Fitzgerald's development what Mizener calls, "a leap forward"? For one thing, given the materials he had to work with, "glorified anecdote" or not, Fitzgerald did a superb job as a craftsman. As Mizener writes,

> He had found a story which allowed him to exploit much
> more of his feeling about experience, and he had committed
> himself to an adequate and workable form which he never
> betrayed.

Furthermore, the story afforded him a chance to utilize his deeply felt relationship with Zelda, as well as his deepseated attitude toward the wealthy.

But for me, it is the language of the novel, its lucid and brilliantly controlled style, that rescues *The Great Gatsby* from being merely another competent novel. In commenting on one of the major flaws of *Gatsby* in another letter to Bishop, Fitzgerald wrote that the weakness was so "astutely concealed . . . by blankets of excellent prose" that no one has noticed it." It is these "blankets of excellent prose" that weave a spell over the reader. (Characteristically, there are six paragraphs that read like an ugly patch on the blanket. They come at the beginning of Chapter Four and are devoted to a farcical description of the leeches who attend Gatsby's parties. The undergraduate humor and satire destroy the tone of the novel here, and I suspect that this section, like Doctor Eckleburg's eyes, was an afterthought.)

In any case, it is the texture of the novel which I wish to examine, for Fitzgerald achieved in *Gatsby* a poetic style which is not found in any of his other novels. Certainly the mature control here is "a leap forward" from the free and easy-going style of the earlier novels. The style of *Tycoon* is as lucid and concentrated, but it is more bare and stripped, and is almost devoid of the kind of integrated imagery employed in *Gatsby*. And it is the novel's imagery, which has been ignored, that I wish to focus on, for I believe that the relationship of imagery and meaning in *Gatsby* is handled with the care and skill of a poet (Fitzgerald wrote verse, not very successfully) and contributes greatly to the enduring success of the novel.

As to the meaning of *The Great Gatsby*, John W. Bichnell has this to say:

> Fitzgerald pronounced a sentence of doom over a social order that imagined itself in full flower. For indeed, the atmosphere, the characterization and the final violence of *Gatsby* all resound with the chords of moral horror and disillusionment.

Further, by the subtle use he makes of the intense heat at the climax of the novel, Fitzgerald suggests that man has taken the rich promise of America and constructed on it a glittering hell. *Gatsby*, like Miller's *Death of a Salesman*, is a bitter indictment of the American dream of success.

Now to the image-clusters that I have alluded to. First, it is clear that Fitzgerald envisioned the world of the rich and corrupt Easterners as a wasteland. East Egg, with its suggestion of life and birth, is, of course, ironic. It is not surprising, then, to discover that he borrowed images from T. S. Eliot's *The Waste Land* to help communicate the sense of desolation and spiritual decay in a land of "stony rubbish," where God has withdrawn and fruitful love seems impossible. Specifically, in Chapter Two Fitzgerald describes Wilson's garage as "a small block of yellow brick sitting on the edge of the waste land . . . contiguous to absolutely nothing. . . . This is a valley of ashes—a fantastic farm where ashes grow like wheat . . . and ash-gray men swarm. . . ."

Here, instead of God observing the actions of the humans involved in the impending tragedy, an occulist's giant advertisement looks down and "broods on over the solemn dumping ground." This sign becomes one of the pervading symbols of the novel and is constantly alluded to—no doubt too often.

Fitzgerald is said to have memorized *The Waste Land*. Indeed, Lionel Trilling has referred to *Gatsby* as a prose version of the poem, certainly an overstatement of the case. Although the prevailing tone of the novel is brooding and elegiac, I cannot find many concrete verbal echoes from the poem. Fitzgerald was content with repeating the waste-land image and expanding the imagery of "the valley of ashes." For example, he alludes to men of ashes, "trail of ashes," and Wilson is covered by "white ashen dust." Daisy echoes the lady in "A Game of Chess" when she cries out in boredom, "What'll we do with ourselves this afternoon . . . and the day after that, and the next thirty years?" The impact of Eliot is clear, but his influence on the imagery of the novel is not really large. (Incidentally, Eliot wrote Fitzgerald that he was tremendously excited by the novel and had read it three times.)

There is another cluster of images that owes nothing to T. S. Eliot. One of Fitzgerald's aims in *The Great Gatsby* was to show the artificiality, the insincerity and the emptiness of Daisy and Tom Buchanan's world—and by extension, the society of the decadent rich of the twenties. As Nick Carroway encounters more and more of this society, like a modern Huck Finn he penetrates beneath the surface brilliance and gaiety until it loses its glamour; and, finally, he retreats, wiser and disillusioned, to a crude, yet moral, West.

An important part of Fitzgerald's method of conveying this hollowness is centered around the repetition of images that suggest a lack of substance. The main characters portrayed in the novel are, like the typical members of the lost generation, drifters; they seem to drift and float without purpose or direction, "like casual moths." *Drift* and *float* are

the two most important verbs in the novel, and it is interesting to note the way Fitzgerald reiterates them like motifs
in a musical composition. Early in the novel he refers to the
"foul dust [that] floated in the wake" of Gatsby's dreams.
Gatsby is said to have drifted out of nowhere. In East Egg
when Nick first meets Daisy and Jordan Baker, the athletic
girl he almost falls in love with, a breeze seems to lift the
women up, as though they were not made of flesh and blood:

> The only completely stationary object in the room was an
> enormous couch on which two young women were buoyed up
> as though upon an anchored balloon. They were both in
> white, and their dresses were rippling and fluttering as if
> they had just been blown back in after a short flight around
> the house.

This is a crucial scene, for Fitzgerald develops and repeats
the basic imagery here, just as he does the valley of ashes
image. Daisy, whose last name is Fay, has lived in a world
as unreal and as amoral as fairyland: "her artificial world
was redolent of orchids and pleasant, cheerful snobbery . . .
where fresh faces drifted here and there like rare petals
blown by the sad horns around the floor." She is also compared to a silver idol, and Gatsby learns, too late, how
futile it is to bow down before idols, and how dangerous it
is to aspire to the King's daughter in the enchanted palace.
At the end of the novel his fairy-princess vanishes, and he is
left "watching over nothing."

But Daisy is not the only one who drifts and floats. As
we have seen, Jordan Baker and Gatsby are described in
similar terms. At the vulgar and drunken party which Tom
Buchanan forces Nick to attend, Myrtle Wilson, Tom's
mistress, "seemed to be revolving in a noisy, creaking pivot
through the smoky air." The image here helps parallel Daisy
and her lower-class rival. Later, feeling alone, Nick reflects,
"unlike Gatsby and Tom Buchanan, I had no girl whose
disembodied face floated along the dark cornices and blind-
ing signs. . . ." And more important, after Daisy has run over
and killed Myrtle Wilson, when Nick arrives, "The Buchan-
ans' house floated suddenly toward us through the dark

rustling trees." I need not recount how the cocktails and inebriated guests float through Gatsby's fabulous parties. Enough has been said to indicate that Fitzgerald's imagery is chosen to suggest an insubstantial world which has torn loose from its moorings following the first World War.

Closely connected with this image-cluster is another group whose function is to suggest, I think, a nightmare quality, a world of frightening and chaotic unreality. Nick remarks that the reports of Gatsby's murder "were a night-mare—grotesque and untrue." Two years later, when he looks back on his fantastic experiences in the East, he is impressed by "a quality of distortion" that was always present, so much so that finally he thinks of his summer in Long Island in terms of "a night scene by El Greco." The truth of the matter is that Fitzgerald's imagery constantly points the reader (who is more aware at first than the callow narrator) to this nightmare quality, until the novel begins to take on the atmosphere of a maddening dream. This technique could have been suggested by *The Waste Land,* but I believe that Fitzgerald borrowed the basic imagery here from Joseph Conrad's *Heart of Darkness,* which I take to be the primary literary source of the novel. In Conrad's story, as Marlow (who is much like Nick) travels up the Congo to meet Kurtz (Gatsby's counterpart) the world be-comes so nightmarish that he begins to doubt its reality, even his own sanity. The people around him become phantoms and wraiths. Of course, much the same thing happens to Nick, though it is not emphasized in the heavy-handed man-ner of Conrad. (Significantly, both Marlow and Nick are initiated into the world of reality by being exposed to a kind of hell.) The deeper Nick gets involved in the East, the more unreal it becomes. The world changes, "just as things grow in fast movies," "women fade through doors into warm darkness," houses float and melt away, characters seem to vanish (Gatsby does this twice), men of ashes "move dimly and already crumbling through the powdery air." Things seem to be bewitched: after his first meeting with Daisy and

Tom, Nick feels "as though the whole evening had been a trick of some sort. . . ." Later, things become even more haunting: Nick observes Myrtle Wilson "walking through her husband as if he were a ghost"; in her apartment a photograph hangs like an ectoplasm. There are other similar allusions, but these are enough to make the point. Through his imagery Fitzgerald is saying that the society he is depicting is not only hollow and insubstantial, but is as grotesque and unreal as a nightmare.

Perhaps one other facet of the imagery in *Gatsby* deserves a passing comment. There is not space here to elaborate on Fitzgerald's use of color imagery, but I might at least note that he handles this poetic device with the skill of Joseph Conrad in *Heart of Darkness* or, say, Crane in the impressionistic *The Red Badge of Courage*—though he does not employ it as extensively as Crane. And, like the animal imagery in Steinbeck's *Of Mice and Men,* Fitzgerald's color images are always a part of his central meaning.

To be more concrete, white is the color most often used. Daisy and Jordan dress in white, Gatsby's guests make love under a white plum tree, his mansion is white in the moonlight, and he is constantly posed on his white marble steps. During the argument between Gatsby and Tom Buchanan at the climax of the novel, Jordan Baker says, "We are all white here." It soon becomes obvious that Fitzgerald is using white ironically; his characters are no more white and innocent than Moby Dick. This ironic use of color is in keeping with the ironic tone of the whole novel. Fitzgerald also uses yellow throughout the story, a color suggesting decay as in Joyce's *Portrait of the Artist as a Young Man* or Eliot's "J. Alfred Prufrock." Just before Gatsby is murdered, for instance, he disappears into yellowing trees, which here foreshadows his death. Also, much is made of green, particularly the green light that Gatsby yearns for on Daisy's dock, which comes to symbolize the "green light" that all Americans believe in. Needless to say, gray is often repeated, in keeping the waste land motif. Gatsby is wearing an absurd pink suit at the climax of the novel, perhaps to symbolize a kind of innocence which he still retains in a decadent society. Much of the rich sensuous quality of the style of *Gatsby* depends on Fitzgerald's masterful use of color imagery. In fact, if one were to analyze the novel as a poem—as well it might be—it would not be inappropriate to label *Gatsby* as Keatsian in its concrete and sensuous imagery.

Perhaps no way of indicating Fitzgerald's artistry in *Gatsby* can be better than quoting a passage where all the types of images discussed here are woven together. The following passage comes after the climax, when Gatsby begins to see the falseness of his dream, just before Wilson murders him. Nick Carroway surmises that Gatsby must have acquired a new orientation when he realized that Daisy was irrevocably lost:

> A new world, natural without being real, where poor ghosts breathing dreams like air, drifted fortuitously about . . . like that ashen, fantastic figure gliding toward him through the amorphous trees.

This is prose of a very high order. Substitute *language* for *art*, and I agree with Mizener when he says of *The Great Gatsby*, "The art of the book is nearly perfect." The art of the novel is far from being perfect, but the language is nearly so. For in *The Great Gatsby* Fitzgerald achieved something his other novels lack: a careful integration of imagery and meaning.

NORTH CAROLINA STATE UNIVERSITY

* Robert Griffin earned his M. A. at the University of Florida, and is currently a Graduate Fellow at the University of California (Berkeley). His articles have been published in several scholarly journals.

Ethical Point of View in "The Sound and the Fury"

I BELIEVE THAT MAN will not merely endure: he will prevail. He is immortal, not because he alone among creatures has an inexhaustible voice, but because he has a soul, a spirit capable of compassion and sacrifice and endurance. The poet's, the writer's, duty is to write about these things. It is his privilege to help man endure by lifting his heart, by reminding him of the courage and honor and hope and pride and compassion and pity and sacrifice which have been the glory of his past. The poet's voice need not merely be the record of man, it can be one of the props, the pillars to help him endure and prevail.

(Faulkner's Nobel Prize Address—Stockholm, 1949)

Since his Stockholm address, critics have paid a good deal of attention to the moral content, the heart-lifting or quasi-religious "message," of William Faulkner's fiction. They have noted that probably every work contains some assertion of value; in *Sanctuary*, for example, it has been observed that the idea of responsibility is championed through vivid depiction of (the perils of) retreat from responsibility. Such authorities as William Van O'Connor have pointed out that one of Faulkner's persistently reiterated themes is that of the prostituted Christian spirit—more precisely, Protestant or Calvinist spirit—in the South. *Light in August* is a case in point. The irony of Joe Christmas' name, and of the time-pattern parallels between his life and Christ's, is universally noted; the major irony is his being always pursued and harassed by voices of "Christian" righteousness. There is, for instance, the sadistic self-righteousness of Joe's mad grandfather, Doc Hines—not to mention Joe's almost equally "saintly" guardian, Simon McEachern, a ruthless puritan who can pray "that Almighty be as magnanimous as himself" in forgiving some trivial disobedience; actually the whole community is found wanting, "since to pity him would be to admit self-doubt and to hope for and need pity themselves." Throughout is the theme of rigidity of spirit as opposed to the need for acceptance of human fallibility and the need for pity and sympathy.

But while Faulkner may often present these ironies of unrealistic religiousness, he also indicates that one may find direction, discipline, and consolations in religion. (In *Light in August* Byron Bunch provides the contrasting norm, as the man who committed himself to the moral life but can still admit self-doubt and demonstrate real charity.) It is this beneficial side of religion which Faulkner emphasizes in *The Sound and the Fury*.

In her excellent analysis, *"The Sound and the Fury:* A Study in Perspective" (*PMLA,* LXIX, December 1954, 1017-37), Olga W. Vickery treats the four-part structure of the novel as representative of four ways of perceiving experience, dramatizing the progression from a private to a public world: Benjy's associative system of sensations, Quentin's obsessive abstractions, Jason's individualistic profit-and-loss pragmatism, and Dilsey's ability to create order out of experience through her tragic awareness of life. I should like to elaborate a little on Mrs. Vickery's analysis; where she concentrates more on the epistemological aspects of the structure, the present discussion focuses on perspectives as *ethical* perspectives, particularly in the light of relationships to Christian religion.

I want to emphasize that *The Sound and the Fury* is a moral book, that integral to its structure is the depiction of four distinct ethical points of view. To outline simply, one may say that the novel presents in turn an amoral report of sensations and reactions, the emotive abstractions of a moral absolutist or "idealist," the rationalizations of a moral hypocrite, and the humanistic acceptance and endurance of a moral realist; thus the progression is ethical as well as epistemological. This is not the whole of Faulkner's meaning, of course, but it does constitute so integral an element that the novel is definitely a moral book, and ultimately a sort of religious book.

To say that the Benjy section presents an ethical point of view may be a bit misleading, for the very importance of the section to this aspect of the novel is the absence of any ethical perspective. Benjy is totally amoral. His reports or remembrances of what-was and what-is are colored by no conception of what-ought-to-be; no value judgments are expressed in his section. His mind receives (and, for the novelist's convenience, gives out) mere sensations connected somehow in space and time but not mentally connected by logical or causal relationships. His thoughts proceed by simple association—generally mnemonic—rather than by an imposed interpretation. Thus he scarcely thinks at all; he does not judge. This does not mean that he has no evaluative reactions; in a sense he does. He may react favorably or unfavorably (e.g., by bellowing), but he does not conceive of his reactions to events as being evaluational. He reacts unfavorably to Caddy's perfume and favorably to her natural tree-like smell, but he does not judge, "perfume is bad." Similarly when he does wrong—molesting the little girl—he does not see it as wrong, because he does not know what wrong is. He does not know wrong from right, because he does not know the concepts *wrong* and *right*. Thus Benjy is the pure innocent, the personification of the amoral point of view.

In the second section, we find Quentin suffering from an altogether different ethical perspective. Quentin is an idealist, insofar as that term denotes one who adheres to moral absolutes or fixed principles. It is true that Quentin is the victim of his own abstractions, but it must be remembered that these are not just theoretic abstractions rationally arrived at. Quentin is very emotional about his abstractions; he is a zealot. Things are either all right or all wrong for him, and when he finds that nothing is altogether right he suffers from his conviction that everything is wrong. He notices the watches in the window of a watchmaker's shop and asks, "Are any of them right?" The watchmaker's "No" reinforces his interpretation of the universe:

> There were about a dozen watches in the window, a dozen different hours and each with the same assertive and contradictory assurance that mine had, without any hands at all. Contradicting one another.

He makes the mistake his father describes as that of "confusing sin and morality," because he believes as his mother says that "there is no halfway ground." Caddy's fiance, Herbert, tells Quentin that "a young fellow like you would consider cheating a lot more serious than you will in five years"; to which Quentin replies, "I don't know but one way to consider cheating I don't think I'm likely to learn different at Harvard." He doesn't learn that there is more than one way, and therein lies his tragedy; he never accepts his father's word that purity "is a negative state and therefore contrary to nature." This fervent, literally suicidal devotion of Quentin's to abstract absolutes Faulkner has underscored in his Appendix to the novel:

> Quentin III. Who loved not his sister's body but some concept of Compson honor. . . . Who loved not the idea of the incest which he could not commit, but some presbyterian concept of its eternal punishment: he, not God, could by that means cast himself and his sister into hell, where he could guard her forever and keep her forevermore intact amid the eternal fires.

This is the ultimate position of the moral absolutist: He sets himself up as God.

No doubt Jason realizes the folly of Quentin's idealistic perspective; Mrs. Compson has observed that Jason "is the only one of my children with any practical sense." Jason is not addicted to any absolute abstractions, nor is he emotively involved with anything other than himself. He lets neither theory nor feeling interfere with his self-interest. Caddy observes, "You never had a drop of warm blood in you." His cold-blooded selfishness is everywhere apparent, as in his business dealings. His employer says, " 'I reckon you'll never be a slave to any business,' . . . . 'Not unless it's Jason Compson's business,' [Jason] says." Jason has been characterized as a "utilitarian," and we might conclude that his ethical position is "realistic," insofar as he conducts himself in accordance with a pragmatic refusal to be hamstrung by theoretic principle or emotive attachment. But Jason does profess to adhere to a certain moral code. He claims, for instance, to care about Miss Quentin's behavior because of the family honor. But we may be sure the main reason he has for trying to prevent her escape is fear of losing the checks Caddy has been sending for her daughter's support. In Jason the "decency and pride" of the original Compsons has degenerated into "vanity and self-pity." Jason is a moral hypocrite. He wants to call in the law when his niece runs off with his money, but a large part of that money was savings from his misappropriation of Caddy's checks. He trusts no one, because he knows no one should trust him. His moral "realism" is a perverted realism—and he is, not altogether unlike his brother Quentin, the victim of an *idée fixe*. The remainder of his life is governed by his sense of being cheated out of a job in Caddy's husband's bank, and then out of the money he had misappropriated in order to make up for that original "injustice." Thus Faulkner's characterization of Jason as the "first sane Compson since before Culloden" is heavy with irony, for the fact that he is "logical," "rational," and "contained" is not enough to make him a worthwhile human being—he is too *self*-contained. (However, Jason is "sane" when compared to his two brothers, the idiot and the suicide.) Jason would seem to be an object lesson in the need for the old verities which Faulkner stressed in his Stockholm address.

Dilsey represents the other side of the coin. Her ethical perspective is unblinkingly realistic. She endures because she has learned to accept life and accommodate to it; and her realistic ethic is humanistic, in contrast with Jason's perverted, selfish pragmatism. Dilsey's quiet accommodation to life is neatly synecdochized in her ability to tell time by the one-handed kitchen clock. She recognizes immediately what the distraught librarian, Melissa Meek, failed to recognize: "she knows Caddy doesn't want to be saved hasn't anything worth being saved for nothing worth being lost that she can lose." But it is not enough to say that Dilsey endures because she knows how to accept and make-the-best. Her acceptance is not stoic acceptance (Faulkner has labeled Jason "stoic"); it is Christian. The Negro Easter service in the last section represents a source of Dilsey's strength. On the way to church she exhibits Christian tolerance in the face of objections to her taking Benjy to the service: "Tell um de good Lawd dont keer whether he smart or not." In the church she exhibits Christian disdain for mere appearances: her daughter Frony expresses the general disappointment over the visiting minister's insignificant appearance, and Dilsey replies, "I've knowed de Lawd to use cuiser tools dan dat." Her premonition of the minister's effectiveness is justified, and at the end of the powerful service she sits bolt upright beside Benjy, refortified in her faith, "crying rigidly and quietly in the annealment and the blood of the remembered Lamb."

Dilsey represents in the novel the ethical norm of Christian humanism. Her fundamental Christianity is contrasted with the other characters' lack of it. When she returns home from the Easter service, Mrs. Compson asks for the Bible that has fallen from her bed.

> Dilsey crossed to the bed and groped among the shadows beneath the edge of it and found the Bible, face down. She smoothed the bent pages and laid the book on the bed again. Mrs. Compson didn't open her eyes. Her hair and the pillow were the same color, beneath the wimple of the medicated cloth she looked like an old nun praying. 'Don't put it there

again,' she said without opening her eyes. 'That's where you put it before. Do you want me to have to get out of bed to pick it up?' Dilsey reached the book across her and laid it on the broad side of the bed, 'You can't see to read, noways,' she said. 'You want me to raise de shade a little?' 'No. Let them alone. Go on and fix Jason something to eat.'

Mrs. Compson is not willing to put forth any effort for her religion. She wants it nearby in case she should need it, but evidently has no awareness of needing it, or of how to use it should she sense the need.

I have already suggested the irreligious aspect of Quentin's absolutist ethical perspective: he places himself in the seat of judgment, failing to heed his father's counsel that "every man is the arbiter of his own virtues but let no man prescribe for another man's well-being." Jason is anti-religious. In the Appendix Faulkner speaks of his "thinking nothing of God one way or the other," but he thinks enough of Him to defy Him.

> From time to time (in his frantic pursuit of Miss Quentin and the stolen money) he passed churches, unpainted frame buildings with sheet iron steeples, surrounded by tethered teams and shabby motorcars, and it seemed to him that each of them was a picket-post where the rear guards of Circumstance peeped fleetingly back at him. 'And damn You, too,' he said, 'See if You can stop me,' thinking of himself, his file of soldiers with the manacled sheriff in the rear, dragging Omnipotence down from His throne, if necessary; of the embattled legions of both hell and heaven through which he tore his way and put his hands at last on his fleeing niece.

These contrasts with Dilsey's simple faith—her deriving strength from her Christianity—indicate Faulkner's approval of a kind of Christian ethic. He does not preach or openly advocate, of course; but he presents Dilsey in such a favorable light, dominating the last ("omniscient - author") section of the novel, as to clearly suggest his own sentiments.

Dilsey represents the "old verities" of Christianity — not Christian rites or theological dogma but the fundamental Christian ethic—forbearance and endurance and love and brotherhood. It is significant that the only real sense of brotherhood emerges in the Negroes' Easter service: "their hearts were speaking to one another in chanting measures beyond the needs of words."

Faulkner uses this scene of the church service as a vivid antithesis to the rest of the novel. There are three elements in the scene which contrast with the elements that make up the existence of the Compsons. Instead of the doom and pointlessness of the Compsons' lives, first of all, the St. Louis preacher offers salvation and hope. He hears "de wailin of women and de evenin lamentations" (like the continual weeping of old Mrs. Compson) ; he sees "de darkness and de death everlastin upon de generations"; but these are superseded by the redemption and hope offered through the crucifixion and resurrection he describes, available to all "whut got de blood and de ricklickshun of de Lamb."

And here is the second set of elements contrasted with the Compson existence: the recollection and the blood. The whole tortured effort of the individual Compsons is one of uncontrolled and damning recollection. Underscored by Faulkner's stream-of-consciousness technique, the maddening, frustrating memories drive the protagonists of the tale to their respective judgments, or even comprise the punishment itself as a manifestation of the curse upon them. Benjy's recollections of Caddy cause him to break out repeatedly in his moanings. Quentin's haunting memory of his adolescence with his sister—especially the recurring scene of Caddy and him in the water—leads him finally to his suicide by drowning. Jason's most punitive memories are just beginning in the final pages of the book, just as the church scene opens. He will have to live the remainder of his life with the frustrating recollection of the robbery by his niece and with the knowledge of his impotence in the face of it. Similarly, the blood of the Compsons is that which constitutes the two-fold instrument of doom. They are doomed by the curse upon them, a curse of blood passed down through generations, expressing itself in feeble-mindedness, insanity, alcoholism and promiscuity, and leading to the complete destruction of the family. Furthermore, they are doomed through their pride in the Compson blood, their extreme awareness of the Compson name.

Juxtaposed to the recollection and blood of the Compsons is that of the religious Negroes. Recollection for them, instead of a tortured memory, becomes an ecstatic mystic experience, a remembering that is not a remembering at all but an initiation into a new depth of emotional and existential experience that sustains them where their own backgrounds and family ties are not sufficient. The blood, of course, is not the cursed blood of a family name or of inherited and damning characteristics, but the redeeming sacrificial "blood of the Lamb" that frees the sinner from obsession with himself. The third set of elements contrasts with the sound and the fury of the Compson clan: it consists of the quietness and peace paradoxically induced by the wild fervor of the religious service and expressed in the Compson idiot. Here, for the only time in the book, Benjy finds peace.

Many have noted the "Christ-figure" aspect of Benjy's role in the novel (33 years old, for instance—shades of Joe Christmas). Dilsey says, "You's de Lawd's chile," and in his unintellectualized suffering he has the inadvertent ability to express the world's suffering. His wailing "was nothing. Just sound. It might have been all time and injustice and sorrow become vocal for an instant"—Quentin's obsession with time, Jason's perverted sense of injustice, Dilsey's genuine loving sorrow. We might at first wonder why the idiot so horrified at the disruption of order in going to the left of the monument should not react similarly to the powerful goings-on of the Easter service. There, however, he is at home in the wordless communion of believers, all for the moment pure and innocent and washed in the blood of the Lamb. "In the midst of the voices and the hands Ben sat, rapt in his sweet blue gaze." Of course Benjy's kind of innocence is impotent; he is, in his total natural ignorance, necessarily areligious as well as amoral; he cannot share. But Faulkner has given us a hopeful contrast in the knowing perspective of Dilsey— loving and long-suffering and washed in the blood of humanistic understanding.

UNIVERSITY OF CALIFORNIA, BERKELEY

• *Educated at the University of Florida and at Stetson University, RICHARD LANGFORD has taught American literature in the English department at Stetson for four years. Professor Langford's particular interest has been Eugene O'Neill.*

Eugene O'Neill: The Mask of Illusion

THOUGH GENERALLY RECOGNIZED as the most important American dramatist of the twentieth century, Eugene O'Neill is misunderstood consistently by his critics. His plays are not the morose, pessimistic view of life that both his admirers and detractors say they are.

For example, Wolcott Gibbs, in a May 11, 1957, *New Yorker* review, says O'Neill writes "about people helplessly waiting for their inevitable destruction." Alan Downer, in his *Fifty Years of American Drama*, comments on "O'Neill's fundamental pessimism" and on the playwright's "picture of life [as] a life without foundation, without creeds or belief." One of the bitterest pictures of O'Neill was offered by Edwin Engel, in *The Haunted Heroes of Eugene O'Neill:* "Both early and late O'Neill demonstrated that the world belongs to the insensitive, unperceptive, unselfconscious brute."

To accuse O'Neill of being a total pessimist—a prophet of doom—is to read him superficially. Usually the gloomy tone in O'Neill is but his way of expressing the tragic consequences that await those who are content with illusions; the gloom is not intended to be understood as an end in itself.

For O'Neill, the tragedy of man lies in the search for spiritual peace among the false gods of ambition, pride,

security, physical love, etc. All of these human goals are unreal to O'Neill; they are the illusions that men live by, to
avoid the difficulties of reality. His dramas are primarily
attempts to depict man in the struggle to distinguish illusion
from reality—attempts to restore man's perspective and offer
him a solution to his predicament.

O'Neill says:

> I'm always acutely conscious of the Force behind— (Fate, God,
> our biological past creating our present, whatever one calls it
> —Mystery, certainly) —and of the one eternal tragedy of Man
> in his glorious, self-destructive struggle to make the Force ex-
> press him instead of being, as an animal is, an infinitesimal
> incident in its expression.

Making "the Force express him" is man's error; it is an in-
version of truth, which leads man to live in a world of illusions, separated from reality by his own egoistic rationalizations.

The tendency of man to take the easy way—to live behind
his illusions—often outrages the dramatist's sense of man's
duty. The reluctance of man even to try — man's childish
satisfaction with fool's gold—occasionally results in what seem
to be bitter denunciations of humanity.

For instance, in *The Iceman Cometh*, Hickey screams
helplessly; "By rights you should be contented now, without
a single damned hope or lying dream left to torment you."
And Yank, in *The Hairy Ape*, said to represent man in his
endless, seemingly pointless agonies, strikes out savagely at
humanity in general on a Sunday morning, on New York's
Fifth Avenue. But what seems to be bitterness on the part of
O'Neill is usually anger directed at those who will not even
try to understand his thesis: that man must discard the com-
forting crutch of illusion if he expects to know any peace of
mind in this world.

If the world were two-valued—all good or all evil—then it
might make sense to place O'Neill in the pessimistic camp.
Despite the fact that the world is likely to be merely a
tenuous, on-going process, most people do orient themselves
in a two-valued manner, if only for the sake of convenience

—and the convenience becomes a snare. As a result of the pressure to label a man in one way or another, O'Neill is made headmaster of the "doom and gloom" school. Thus, many critics who are generally sensitive and percipient find nothing but pessimism in him.

But O'Neill reserves the traditional right of genius to be an innovator—to see the world in a unique way. As Joseph Wood Krutch said, in *Theatre Arts*, October, 1954:

> What the lonely O'Neill discovered was that neither modern optimism nor modern pessimism corresponded to his own experience or to his own vision. On the one hand, man's unhappiness was not simply the result of social maladjustment. On the other hand, these sorrows are not merely the ignoble thing which pessimistic naturalism makes of them.

The responsible artist is not blindly optimistic, nor is he futilely pessimistic; he must seek a form of expression which recognizes reality (what man is), and concurrently offers man some conception of the ideal (what man can become). From the need for such a form comes O'Neill's expressionism.

O'Neill tries to lift the audience above its ordinary thought patterns so that he may reveal a truth, while the mind of the audience is clear and perceptive. He tries to cut away symbolically what he called "the banality of surfaces," deliberately destroying dramatic conventions, if necessary, to surprise his audience into seeing reality.

Men often mistake a label for an object—a name for a thing which the name only represents. Dramatic expressionism becomes O'Neill's way to suspend the operation of what man calls reality (illusion) so that man may be shown the truth that lies just beneath the surface. Often O'Neill shows the onlooker only the essence of what he usually thinks of as reality, then points out that the "reality" is only an illusion—a label—and is not real at all.

In *The Hairy Ape,* Yank is not portrayed as a real person; he is an expressionistic abstraction, representing all workers who are denied an opportunity to develop individual personalities. The illusion-Yank is free to remove surfaces and point out truths. He piques the curiosity—as a symbol, he permits the audience to empathize with him in his attempts to rise out of the class (label) society has placed him in.

Another clear example of the effectiveness of O'Neill's expressionism is in *The Emperor Jones*. The playgoer sees "little formless fears" scurrying around on stage, taunting Jones. Jones sees them—and reacts to them—as if they were real; but the audience sees them as illusions. Everyone understands that the fears are merely the product of Jones' over-active imagination. However, the point is that the same audience ordinarily reacts to those fears as if they were real, in their own lives; that is, until O'Neill lifts the veil and permits them to see what he called "the behind life."

The expression — the theatrical device of illusion — becomes a way to trick the audience into seeing truth. What begins as a stage-illusion becomes a life-reality, far closer to truth than the stereotyped labels attached to life by most individuals. Often unrecognized and sometimes ignored, reality is with us constantly; but it takes an O'Neill to depict the common in an uncommon manner, and thus allow us a glimpse of truth.

In his major dramas O'Neill is concerned pointedly with this conflict between illusion and reality. The key is found in the one major character, in almost every play, who sheds his illusions. One character gains insight, and at least begins to live with things as they are.

For example, in *The Straw*, Stephen faces reality—too late as far as the girl he loves is concerned, but not too late for him to understand the hypocrisy of his own position. In *The First Man*, a scientist surrenders his illusion of anticipated professional status to become a father to a child he had not wanted. In *A Touch of the Poet*, Con Melody destroys a horse that had become the symbol of his egoistic pride, and re-orients himself in terms of his real self, assuming the responsibilities of his family and business. And in *The Ice-*

man Cometh, Larry sits in his chair at the play's conclusion, "born condemned to see both sides of a question," unable to lose himself in drink; he must see things as they are.

Only the realist, then, can find truth; only the realist—who does not succumb to the "little formless fears" of this world—has a chance.

When asked why he did not write happier plays, O'Neill replied:

> Sure I'll write about happiness if I can happen to meet up with that luxury, and find it sufficiently dramatic and in harmony with any deep rhythm in life. But happiness is a word. What does it mean? Exaltation; an intensified feeling of the significant worth of man's being and becoming? Well, if it means that — and not a mere smirking contentment with one's lot — I know there is more of it in real tragedy than in all the happy-ending plays ever written. It's mere present-day judgment to think of tragedy as unhappy!
>
> A work of art is always happy; all else is unhappy. . . . I don't love life because it's pretty. Prettiness is only clothes-deep. I am a truer lover than that, I love it naked. There is beauty to me even in its ugliness.

.   .   .   .

Note that "a work of art is always happy." Art is happy because it states truths and dispels illusions. Art assists man in clearing away the myriad mists of conventional life, behind which man hides his true nature. Any work of art is happy, not pessimistic, if it makes a genuine effort to extricate man from his illusions, and to assist him in the process of "being and becoming."

Two O'Neill dramas that are very often misinterpreted are *A Moon for the Misbegotten* and *Long Day's Journey Into Night.* The former is actually a sequel to the latter, though the sequel was published first. Both plays are largely autobiographical. Though each will stand alone artistically, they are best considered with their relationship in mind.

James Tyrone, Jr., in *Moon,* represents O'Neill's older brother. The play tells of the alcoholic degeneration of Tyrone, and of the compassion and understanding of Josie, who lives with her father, Hogan, in a tenant farmhouse on Tyrone's estate. Josie, in love with Tyrone, schemes with Hogan to trap Tyrone into marrying her. She says, determinedly, "Do you think I'm lying? Just give me a chance. . . ."

Tyrone knows Josie is a better person than she pretends to be. He knows her constant boasting about various love affairs is only an attempt to maintain her pride in the face of scorn from the community.

Tyrone does not want Josie to succumb to his drunken attentions; he wants her to remain an ideal of womanhood in his mind. Only by re-affirming his faith in Josie's purity can Tyrone find the strength to continue his personal battle to "belong."

Josie's immoral scheme collapses; she fails deliberately to take advantage of Tyrone when the opportunity arises. Tyrone's faith in Josie—and in life—is sustained, and both Josie and Hogan see clearly that life is not to blame for their unhappiness. Josie's father says: "It was life I was cursing—or maybe I was cursing myself for a damned old scheming fool, like I ought to." Josie replies: "Look out. I might say Amen to that." Having shed the illusion that conformity to village morality is a vital goal, Josie can live at peace with herself.

Wolcott Gibbs, reviewing *A Moon for the Misbegotten* in *The New Yorker of* May 11, 1957, says: "It is quite possible, I suppose, to regret her [Josie's] immediate romantic and domestic trials, but very difficult to despair of her future." He goes on to say: "The fact that there is no real reason to suppose that the defeated Josie will be defeated at all does away with approximately half of O'Neill's point. . . ."

The fact does not really negate any part of O'Neill's point. In both of his statements, Gibbs makes the same mistake made by so many who read nothing but cynicism and bitterness into O'Neill's plays. Josie has faced reality and won—she has determined to live without the facade of pride that had kept her from becoming herself. One finds it "difficult to despair of her future" because she is now a stronger person. O'Neill's point is actualy strengthened by Gibbs' faulty observations, because the point to *Moon* is not Josie's defeat, but her triumph. And though he is erroneous in his conclusion, Gibbs obviously sees that Josie *has* triumphed. O'Neill shows that truth—and beauty—can be found anywhere, even in the squalor of a tenant farmhouse occupied by a frustrated girl and her drunken father.

When *Moon* is understood, it is not the gloomy play that many critics think it is. All three of the main characters face truth and realize the foolishness of measuring happiness against conventional standards only. Each decides to live as an individual, assuming the obligation to be patient with life and to try to comprehend and cope with the special predicament each of their lives presents.

As for *Long Day's Journey Into Night,* many think it leaves absolutely no hope for man. However, if one considers the play as a complete work of art, instead of as a series of distressing emotional episodes, one finds it to be a hopeful affirmation of O'Neill's belief that man can find a way out of the dilemma in which he exists.

Based on the dramatist's early life, *Journey* describes the emotional difficulties of the author (Edmund), his brother (James Tyrone, Jr.), his mother (Mary), and his father (Tyrone, Sr.). The audience sees these four people caught in a web of frustration and misery which is as much their own weaving as it is fate's.

Edmund, not entirely captured by illusion, is sick; the play ends as he is sent to a TB hospital. James is an alcoholic, almost hopelessly caught in despair, but still trying to find his own purpose in life and to extricate himself from his predicament by placing his faith in his mother's ability to cure herself of dope addiction. He thinks that if his mother can win her battle with dope, then perhaps there is a chance for him to win his with alcohol. The older man, Tyrone, Sr., is a retired actor who lives a life of self-justification. His wealth is known to all of them, but he continues the pretense of poverty almost to the point of causing Edmund's death.

The four confront bitterly what appears to be a hopeless existence. Mary, excusing her weakness, says:

> None of us can help the things life has done to us. They're done before you realize it, and once they're done they make you do other things until at last everything comes between you and what you'd like to be and you've lost your true self forever.

Overhearing an argument between Edmund and Tyrone, Jr., she admonishes Edmund: "It's wrong to blame your brother. He can't help being what the past has made him. Any more than your father can. Or you. Or I."

Edmund cannot stomach such talk; he holds out for more meaning in life than his mother or brother does:

> They never come back! Everything is in the bag! It's all a frame-up! We're all fall guys and suckers and we can't beat the game! Christ, if I felt the way you do—!

Arguing with his father, Edmund tells him: "Yes, facts don't mean a thing, do they? What you want to believe, that's the only truth!" Edmund tells his father of the understanding of life which he has acquired slowly, in his travels around the world. In a lengthy and important soliloquy, he explains his search for and finding of reality:

> I was set free! I belonged, without past or future, within peace and unity and a wild joy, within something greater than my own life, or the life of Man, to Life itself!

When illusions of his own greatness are relinquished, man can understand that he is only "an incident in [the] expression" of "the Force behind," and is not the originator of that force. Edmund describes the peace of mind that came with the acceptance of his own insignificance:

> Then the moment of ecstatic freedom came. The peace, the end of the quest, the last harbor, the joy of belonging to a fulfillment beyond men's lousy, pitiful, greedy fears and hopes and dreams.

Edmund sheds illusions—the masks behind which men hide their true natures—and sees things as they are: "Like the veil of things as they seem drawn back by an unseen hand.

For a second you see—and seeing the secret, are the secret. For a second there is meaning!"

Old Tyrone is moved by his son's sincere, emotionally charged words and says, confessing his own guilt: "I've never admitted this to anyone before, lad, but tonight I'm so heart-sick I feel at the end of everything, and what's the use of false pride and pretense." He explains that he could have been a great actor, but he gave up and accepted a highly remunerative, stereotyped role; he realizes that his life has been nothing more than a long series of rationalizations. Finally, he asks Edmund: "What the hell was it I wanted to buy, I wonder, that was worth—well, no matter." Worth his soul? The old actor had sold his soul for a handful of illusions.

Letting go his rationalizations, seeing things clearly, James Tyrone, Sr., can say now: "There's nothing wrong with life. It's we who . . ." Old Hogan has said almost the same thing, in *Moon.* O'Neill is reiterating his basic theme: the man who mistakes form for substance, cheats himself.

All four characters gather for the final scene. Even James, Jr., confesses his guilt: he is jealous of Edmund and tells his younger brother how he has tried to corrupt him. Only Mary, the mother, is left alone in her drugged illusions. She enters, looking desperately around the room for something she says she has lost:

> Something I need terribly. I remember when I had it I was never lonely nor afraid. I can't have lost it forever, I would die if I thought that. Because then there would be no hope.

Mary has lost her faith and searches for it among memories of her youth:

> . . . so I went to the shrine and prayed to the Blessed Virgin and found peace again because I know she heard my prayer and would always love me and see no harm ever came to me so long as I never lost faith in her. That was in the winter of senior year. Then in the spring something happened to me. Yes, I remember. I fell in love with James Tyrone and was so happy for a time.

Mary has spoken the closing lines of *Journey*. O'Neill concludes this powerful play with the central idea implanted firmly in the mind of his audience: Mary has exchanged her spiritual faith for human love—a love that is a temporal illusion. When she married James Tyrone, she saw things as she wanted them to be, not as they were.

The rest of the family can no longer place faith in Mary. Each of them must face the truth; each must seek moral strength for himself. All hope for Mary's recovery is gone, and the play appears to end sadly.

But hope stems from the other characters, from their expressions of guilt and their decisions to accept responsibility for their actions. There is hope in the fact that three men face each other and speak the truth. And there is hope in the fact that James, Jr., will continue to try to "beat the game," as he transfers that desire from a dependence on Mary to an emotionally more acceptable relationship with Josie, in *Moon*.

The sadness and frustrations that envelop the characters in *Long Day's Journey Into Night* are to be considered as stepping stones to reality, not as indications of man's certain doom. O'Neill expresses in the play his understanding of man's position in relation to his creator: he portrays characters who face defeating human problems, but who become aware that human problems— and human joys—will end. Three characters in *Journey* face their dilemma and determine to go on trying to understand themselves and their world. It isn't that all men are doomed, says O'Neill—but some are: those who do not wish to see the truth, and will not try. For these, there is only the false, immoral comfort of dreams.

As Stark Young has said:

> More than any other of our playwrights he was concerned, as he said himself, not with plays about man's relation to man, but with man's relation to something larger than man and beyond him.

Often torn between a desire to make God into a man and a desire to touch a spiritual something beyond man, O'Neill suffered the emotional anguish of all who search for a valid ultimate meaning for man's existence. Some of his searching is scarred by cynicism, as many critics have noted, but most of it is marked with genuine love—not of what man is—but of what man can become. His dramas are positive, noble expressions of one man's understanding of the human dilemma. With a genius for comprehending man's nature, and with compassion for man's failures, Eugene O'Neill affirms man's hope for meaning and beauty in life.

STETSON UNIVERSITY

• J. P. HUNTER *was an ad writer and a reporter be-fore he became a teacher; now he serves as an editorial assistant for* STUDIES IN ENGLISH LITERATURE, *and is on the bibliography staff of* TWENTIETH CENTURY LITERATURE. *He took his several degrees at Miami University, the University of Florida, and Rice University. In the fall of 1962, he will be teaching literature at Williams College.*

Steinbeck's Wine of Affirmation in "The Grapes of Wrath"

IT HAS BEEN A LONG TIME since John Steinbeck won the Drama Critics' Circle Award (1937) and the Pulitzer Prize (1939), and many of the critics who liked his work then have recently found lit-tle to praise. Since World War II, Steinbeck's new novels have received increasingly harsh reviews, and his critical reputation has declined steadily. Many of his most ardent admirers are now no longer confident that he will achieve the eminence once predicted for him, and some of them despair that he will ever do important work again. Now Steinbeck's decreasing stature seems to be reflected in another way—a growing tendency to find his later failures anticipated in his earlier work.

A few years ago it was popular to speculate on "what had happened" to Steinbeck, and some interesting answers were proposed: Steinbeck had lost touch with the country and with California, and the new urban and urbane life of New York was insufficient to fill his well; the death of Edward Ricketts (his close friend) had been such a personal blow to Steinbeck that his creative powers were affected; Steinbeck's ideology had changed, and the new Steinbeck had nothing to say; success had "spoiled" Steinbeck. However, even though some of these answers are still being given, an increasing number of critics seem to be turning to an answer given long ago by Steinbeck's detractors: that no decline in fact exists, that Steinbeck's talents, in his earlier period, were simply overrated by those who believed in the causes Steinbeck championed. One suspects that we may hear more and more of this point of view unless Steinbeck produces a new work of distinction. Once, much of the early work—certainly *The Grapes of Wrath* and *Of Mice and Men,* and possibly *In Dubious Battle* and several short pieces—seemed certain of a place in American fiction; now, it seems necessary to restate their claim to attention. Some of these pieces—especially the "worker" novels—are still taught in the college classroom, but already (despite the work of such critics as Peter Lisca and Warren French) there is danger of their becoming known as period pieces; again (as when it first appeared) Steinbeck's work needs to be defended as art rather than sociology.

I

Almost everyone agrees that *The Grapes of Wrath* is Steinbeck's most important early work, and it may well be that his critical reputation will ultimately stand or fall on that one book. Those who do not like the novel contend that it exemplifies Steinbeck's most blatant artistic weaknesses: lack of character development, imperfect conception of structure, careless working out of theme, and sentimentality. The last two chapters of the novel have been considered especially illustrative of these weaknesses, for they are said to demonstrate the final inability of Steinbeck to come to grips, except in a superficial way, with the ideological and artistic problems posed in the novel. The final scene has drawn the sharpest criticism of all, for here Steinbeck is charged with a sensational, shocking, and therefore commercial substitute for an artistic solution. The charges are not new ones, but they have a peculiar urgency at a time when the reputation of Steinbeck's early work is in danger of eclipse. And they constitute a basal attack on Steinbeck as artist, for if it is true that his most important book is inadequately conceived and imperfectly worked out, Steinbeck's claim to a place among significant novelists is seriously impaired.

The inadequacy of the ending of *The Grapes of Wrath,* is, however, more apparent than real. When the events of the last two chapters (and particularly the final scene in the barn) are examined in relation to the novel's total structure, they demonstrate a careful working out of theme in fictional terms. At the end, the Joads who remain (only six of the original twelve) seem to have a grim physical future; as they hover in a dry barn while the deluge continues and the waters rise, they face the prospect of a workless winter in a hostile world. But even though their promised land has turned out to be " 'no lan' of milk and honey' " but instead a battleground stained with the blood of Jim Casy, the Joads are at last able to come to grips with their world. Instead of idealists who dream of white houses and clusters of plenty they have become people of action who translate the prophecy of Jim Casy into the realities of wrath.

II

Under the old order in Oklahoma, the Joads were a proud people, individualists who asked nothing from anyone and who were content with their family-size world as long as they had a home surrounded by land which they could caress into fertility. Like the early Tom, they believed in " 'Just puttin' one foot in front a the other,' " and their thoughts did not stray beyond the limits of their families and their land. When the change comes, when they find themselves in captivity on land they have known as their own, and finally when the captor banks insult their dignity by driving them like nomads away from their homes, they do not understand the change, and they are helpless to oppose it. A few, like Muley Graves, may try, pitifully, to fight back with a sniper's bullet or a harassing laugh from parched fields, but the majority only know that the old is gone, and that they are powerless to fight against the new. As the dust covers the land and the burrowing machines cut their swath of progress through fields and houses, the men stand figuring in the dust, unbroken by events, but powerless to change them.

In their powerlessness, the Joads and their neighbors first choose the road of illusion, and they pursue their particular Western version of the American dream across Route 66. In their heads dance visions of plenty in California — their Canaan of the Golden West — but their map is an orange handbill, and soon their luxurious dreams of ripe fruit and white houses are changed to nightmares of hunger and Hoovervilles. Even in California, the Joads are merely individuals driven by forces they do not understand until, in wrath, they learn their lesson.

The lesson they learn forms the thematic base of *The Grapes of Wrath,* and although the Joads do not accept it fully until the end of the novel, the solution has been suggested quite early in the narrative. This theme—that strength can be achieved through a selfless unity of the entire community of Dispossessed—is first suggested when Tom and Jim Casy meet Muley Graves, a kind of mad prophet, on the old Joad place, and Muley is asked whether he will share his food. " 'I ain't got no choice in the matter,' " Muley says, then explains:

> 'That ain't like I mean it. That ain't. I mean'—he stumbled —'what I mean, if a fella's got somepin to eat an' another fella's hungry—why, the first fella ain't got no choice. I mean, s'pose I pick up my rabbits an' go off somewheres an' eat 'em. See?
> 'I see,' said Casy. 'I can see that. Muley sees somepin there, Tom. Muley's got a-holt of somepin and it's too big for him, an' it's too big for me.'

Though he still doesn't understand the concept fully, Casy has already incorporated Muley's prophetic wisdom into his own wilderness philosophy when, during his breakfast "grace" (two chapters later), he tells of his insights:

'I got thinkin' how . . . mankin' was holy when it was one thing. An' it on'y got unholy when one mis'able little fella got the bit in his teeth an' run off his own way, kickin' an' draggin' and fightin'. Fella like that bust the holiness. But when they're all workin' together, not one fella for another fella, but one fella kind of harnessed to the whole shebang— that's right, that's holy.'

Later Casy develops the idea and translates it into action, ultimately even sacrificing himself for it. But at first he finds few hearers. At breakfast, Ma is the only one who seems to notice the unusual "prayer," and she watches Casy "as though he were suddenly a spirit, not human any more, a voice out of the ground." The other Joads listen to Casy, but they do not hear him for a long time.

III

Casy's role is central to the structure of *The Grapes of Wrath,* for in him the narrative structure and the thematic structure are united. This role is best seen when set against the Biblical background which informs both types of structure in the novel. Peter Lisca has noted that the novel reflects the three-part division of the Old Testament exodus account (captivity, journey, promised land), but that the "parallel is not worked out in detail." Actually, the lack of detailed parallel seems to be deliberate, for Steinbeck is reflecting a broader background of which the exodus story is only a part.

Steinbeck makes the incidents in his novel suggest a wide range of Old and New Testament stories. As the twelve Joads (corresponding to the twelve tribes of Israel) embark on their journey (leaving the old order behind), they mount the truck in ark fashion, two by two:

> . . . the rest swarmed up on top of the load, Connie and Rose of Sharon, Pa and Uncle John, Ruthie and Winfield, Tom and the preacher. Noah stood on the ground looking up at the great load of them sitting on top of the truck.

Grampa (like Lot's wife) is unable to cope with the thought

of a new life, and his wistful look at the past brings his death—a parallel emphasized by the scripture verse (quoting Lot) which Tom picks out to bury with Grampa. Uncle John (like Ananias) withholds money from the common fund, in order to satisfy his selfish desires. The list could be lengthened extensively, and many allusions are as isolated and apparently unrelated to the context as the ones cited here. Looked at in one way, these allusions seem patternless, for they refer to widely separated sections of Biblical history. However, the frequency of allusion suggests the basic similarity between the plight of the Joads and that of the Hebrew people. Rather than paralleling a single section of Biblical history, the novel reflects the broader history of the chosen people from their physical bondage to their spiritual release by means of a messiah.

If the reader approaches *The Grapes of Wrath* searching for too exact a parallel, he will be disappointed, for just when it seems as if a one-to-one ratio exists, Steinbeck breaks the pattern. Tom, for example, is a Moses-type leader of his people as they journey toward the promised land. Like Moses, he has killed a man and has been away for a time before rejoining his people and becoming their leader. Like Moses, he has a younger brother (Aaron-Al) who serves as a vehicle for the leader (spokesman-truck driver). And shortly before reaching the destination, he hears and rejects the evil reports of those who have visited the land (Hebrew "spies"—Oklahomans going back). But soon the parallel ends. Carried out carefully at the beginning, it does not seem to exist once the journey is completed. Granma, not Tom, dies just before the new land is reached, and Tom remains the leader of the people until finally (and here a different parallel is suggested) he becomes a disciple of Casy's gospel. This, in the miniature of one character, is what continually happens in *The Grapes of Wrath*. The scene changes, the parallel breaks; and gradually the context shifts from a basically Old Testament one to a New Testament one.

Steinbeck makes his allusions suggestive, rather than exhaustive, and he implies certain parallels without calling for too rigid an allegorical reading. In *East of Eden* Steinbeck also uses the method of suggestive allusion, and Adam's sons are not named Cain and Abel, but Caleb and Aaron (note the initials game again). This is no mere puzzle or covering of tracks, for the method serves to nullify too literal a reading, while at the same time drawing in a whole new range of suggestions. Instead of only Abel, the reader is asked to recall also the Biblical characteristics of another No. 2 brother. In *The Grapes of Wrath,* the method gives Steinbeck the freedom to skirt the particularly vexing time problem, for in the background myth the changes in the Hebrew people take place over centuries, while similar ideological changes in Steinbeck's characters occur within one year. In effect, Steinbeck collapses several hundred years of Hebrew history into the single year of his story; the entire history of man (according to the Judeo-Christian tradition) is reflected in the long hungry summer of one persecuted family.

This span of centuries is focused in Casy, whose ideas bridge the gap from Old to New Testament (according to the Christian concept of Biblical thought as developmental). Parallels between the life of Jim Casy and the messiah whose initials he bears are plentiful. He embarks upon his mission after a long period of meditation in the wilderness; he corrects the old ideas of religion and justice; he selflessly sacrifices himself for his cause, and when he dies he tells his persecutors, " 'You don' know what you're a-doin'.' " Less obvious perhaps, but equally important, is the role of the old Casy, before his wilderness experience, for he must ultimately be considered in messianic rather than Christological terms. Casy had been a typical hell-and-damnation evangelist who emphasized the rigidity of the old moral law and who considered himself ultimately doomed because human frailty prevented his achieving the purity demanded by the law. His conversion to a social gospel represents a movement from Old Testament to New Testament thought, an expanded horizon of responsibility. The annunciation of Casy's message and mission sets the ideological direction of the novel before the journey begins (just as the messiah concept influences Jewish thought for centuries before New Testament times), but only gradually does Casy make an impression upon a people (Jews-Joads) used to living under the old dispensation. Over Route 66 he rides quietly— a guest, a thirteenth—and only as time passes does the new idea blossom and the new order emerge; and the outsider— the thirteenth—becomes spiritual leader of a people to whom he had been a convention, a grace before meals.

Steinbeck's canvas is, on the surface, a painting of broad modern strokes, but its scenes are sketched along the outlines of the Judeo-Christian myth, a sort of polyptych depicting man's sojourn in a hostile world. The background is often faded, sometimes erased, and occasionally distorted, but structurally and ideologically it provides depth for Steinbeck's modern microcosm. In *The Grapes of Wrath* the background ideology becomes secularized and transcendentalized, but the direction of thought is still recognizable: a widening of concern. After the dispersion, there is still a saving remnant whose compassion begins to extend beyond its own familial or tribal group.

Steinbeck's method is perhaps not uniformly successful, and in some work done in this manner (such as *East of Eden* and *Burning Bright*) the fusion of the particular and the mythic seems, if not less perfectly conceived, less carefully wrought. But in *The Grapes of Wrath* the modern and mythic are peculiarly at one, and the story of a family which, in the values of its contemporary society, is hardly worth a jod, is invested with meaning when viewed against a history of enduring signficance.

IV

Casy's gospel is reinforced thematically in *The Grapes of Wrath* by the panoramic intercalary chapters, which translate the plight of the Joad family into larger terms. Structurally, these chapters usually anticipate (in general terms) the particular actions which follow, and stylistically they often recall the King James Bible, particularly the prophetic books such as Isaiah and Jeremiah. Thematically, the most significant of these essays is Chapter 14, which begins:

> The western land nervous under the beginning change. The Western States, nervous as horses before a thunder storm. The great owners, nervous, sensing a change, knowing nothing of the nature of the change.

Later the nature of the change is described:

> One man, one family driven from the land; this rusty car creaking along the highway to the west. I lost my land, a single tractor took my land. I am alone and I am bewildered. And in the night one family camps in a ditch and another family pulls in and the tents come out. The two men squat on their hams and the women and children listen. . . . Here 'I lost my land' is changed; a cell is split and from its splitting grows . . . 'we lost *our* land.' . . . Two men are not as lonely and perplexed as one. And from this first 'we' there grows a still more dangerous thing: 'I have a little food' plus 'I have none.' If from this problem the sum is 'We have a little food,' the thing is on its way, the movement has direction. Only a little multiplication now, and this land, this tractor are ours. . . . This is the beginning—from 'I' to 'we.'

The intercalary chapters record this movement in the novel's action; similar passages in Chapters 1 and 29 (as Lisca has suggested) emphasize the change from family units to larger groupings:

> 1: The people came out of their houses. . . . Men stood by their fences. . . . The men were silent and they did not move often. And the women came out of the houses to stand beside their men—to feel whether this time the men would break. The women studied the men's faces secretly. . . . After a while the faces of the watching men lost their bemused perplexity and became hard and angry and resistant. Then the women knew they were safe and that there was no break.

> 29: The women watched the men, watched to see whether the break had come at last. The women stood silently and

watched. And *where a number of men gathered together,* the fear went from their faces, and anger took its place. And the women sighed with relief, for they knew it was all right— the break had not come; and the break would never come as long as fear could turn to wrath. (Italics mine)

Though the movement from "I" to "we" is imaged several times throughout *The Grapes of Wrath,* the Joads do not really commit themselves to the new mode of thought until very late in the novel. Before their belated commitment, they show their limited view in many ways. Al cannot understand the men's cooperation in job-hunting: " 'Wouldn' it be better,' " he asks, " 'if one fella went alone? Then if they was one piece of work a fella'd get it,' " and he is told:

'You ain't learned . . . . Takes gas to get roun' the country. Gas costs fifteen cents a gallon. Them four fellas can't take four cars. So each of 'em puts in a dime an' they get gas. You got to learn.'

Rose of Sharon and Connie think only of themselves and of now they will break from the group, and when difficulties arise Connie wishes that he had stayed in Oklahoma to man a tractor driving the people from the land. Later, alone, Rose of Sharon complains of her plight and frets about the coming child, and instead of sharing the family responsibility she adds to family worries. Uncle John is similarly preoccupied with his guilt and his personal problems and is almost useless to the group, picking cotton at only half the rate of the other men. Both he and Al withhold money from the family treasury. Noah, thoughtless of the others, wanders away. Connie, leaving a pregnant wife, also deserts. Even the children show a teasing selfishness. Ruthie eats her crackerjacks slowly so that she can taunt the other children when theirs is gone, and at croquet she ignores the rules and tries to play by herself.

Even though Ma, Pa, and Tom are less individualistic than the others, their concern is limited to the family group. Ma's one aim is keeping the family together, and when she says " 'This here fambly's goin' under,' " she is lamenting the disintegration of her entire world. While not a dynamic leader, Pa does his best to fulfill his patriarchal responsibility. Tom shows that he values the family over himself by breaking parole to make the journey with them, and he frequently demonstrates his dedication to them. Once, Tom wishes he could act like Al, but he is unable to forget his responsibility. Ma describes him well: " 'Everything you do is more'n you,' " she says.

Conversion to a wider concern comes rapidly toward the end of *The Grapes of Wrath*. Tom is the first Joad to extend his vision. In wrath, he moves to commitment beside the broken body of Jim Casy. A few days later, when he meets Ma in the dark cave, his dedication is complete. By contrast with Muley Graves (whose womb-like cave is an escape, a place where he feels " 'like nobody can come at me,' ") Tom does not plan to stay in his refuge. He tells Ma of his meditations about Casy and recites a passage Casy had quoted from Ecclesiastes (The Preacher) :

> 'Two are better than one, because they have a good reward for their labor. For if they fall, the one will lif' up his fellow, but woe to him that is alone when he falleth, for he hath not another to help him up. . . . Again, if two lie together, then they have heat; but how can one be warm alone? And if one prevail against him, two shall withstand him, and a three-fold cord is not quickly broken.'

Tom has to leave the family to protect them, but by now he also has a more important reason. He has seen the folly of a narrow family devotion like that of tractor-driver Willy Feely (" 'Fust an' on'y thing I got to think about is my own folks. What happens to other folks is their look-out.' ") and plans to work for a cause transcending family lines:

> 'Tom,' [Ma] said. 'What you aimin' to do?'
> He was quiet for a long time. . . .
> 'Tom,' Ma repeated, 'what you gonna do?'
> 'What Casy done,' he said.

Ma does not fully comprehend Tom's intention, but she has moved from a rigid defense of family unity during the journey (refusing to allow the family to split into two parts: " 'All we got is the family unbroke' ") to acceptance of new ideas in a new order. And after she leaves Tom she is tempted to reach backward—she takes "three steps toward the mound of vines"—but then quickly returns to the camp. Back in the boxcar, Pa talks wistfully of the past times (" 'spen' all my time a thinkin' how it use' ta be' "), but Ma is acclimated to the difference now. " 'This here's purtier—better lan',' " says Ma. Women, she observes, can adapt themselves to change. Earlier, before her meeting with Tom, she had lamented the breakup of the family; now she has a broader perspective: " '*People* is goin' on—changin' a little maybe, but goin' right on.' " Later, she is even more explicit. " 'Use ta be the fambly was fust. It ain't so now. It's anybody.' "

At the time of the birth, the larger unity is demonstrated. Pa (who had said earlier that he would work for twenty cents an hour even if it cost someone else his job) suddenly becomes a leader of men, conscious of the strength of organized effort:

> 'Water's risin',' he said. 'How about if we throwed up a bank? We could do her if ever'body helped.'

The dam is for the Joads, of course, but it is also for the others; all the families face the same danger, and each can flee—alone—or work together for their salvation, and they decide to stay:

> Over the men came a fury of work, a fury of battle. When one man dropped his shovel, another took it up.

Uncle John, choosing between desertion and devotion, works so hard that Pa has to caution him: " 'You take it easy. You'll kill yaself.' " And later, asked to dispose of the baby's body, Uncle John hesitates, then accedes:

> 'Why do I got to do it? Why don't you fellas? I don' like it.' And then, 'Sure. I'll do it. Sure, I will. Come on give it to me.' His voice began to rise. 'Come on! Give it to me.'

Al, whose only concern had been a good time, also moves toward what is, for him, an acceptance of larger responsibility (marriage to Aggie). Even Ruthie, on a child level, shows a change. On the way to the barn, she refuses to share the petals of her flower with Winfield, and, commanded to share, cruelly jabs one petal on his nose; but in her childish way she also senses that times are different:

> Ruthie felt how the fun was gone. 'Here,' she said. 'Here's some more. Stick some on your forehead.'

And, then, in Rose of Sharon, the final change.

V

Rose of Sharon's sacrificial act represents the final breakdown of old attitudes, and climaxes the novel's thematic movement. The final bastion of the old order, Rose of Sharon had been the most selfish of the remaining Joads; her concern had never extended beyond herself and her immediate family (Connie and the expected child). In giving life to the stranger (symbolically, she gives body and wine: Song of Songs 7:7—"Thy breasts [are like] to clusters of grapes"), she accepts the larger vision of Jim Casy, and her commitment fulfills the terms of salvation according to Casy's plan. In their hesitancy and confusion in the old times, the Joads had been powerless to change their fate. Unlike the turtle who dragged through the dust and planted the seeds of the future, they had drawn figures in the dust impotently with sticks. Now, however, they too are purposeful and share the secret of giving life.

The Biblical myth informs the final scene through a cluster of symbols which emphasize the change and affirm the new order. As the Joads hover in the one dry place in their world—a barn—the Bible's three major symbols of a purified order are suggested: the Old Testament deluge, the New Testament stable, and the continuing ritual of communion. In the fusion of the three, the novel's mythic background, ideological progression, and modern setting are brought together; Mt. Ararat, Bethlehem, and California are collapsed into a single unit of time, and life is affirmed in a massive symbol of regeneration.

The novel's final picture—a still life of Rose of Sharon holding the old man—combines the horror with the hope. Its imitation of the madonna and child (one face mysteriously smiling; the other wasted, and with wide, frightened eyes) is a grotesque one, for it reflects a grotesque world without painless answers, a world where men are hit by axe handles and children suffer from skitters. Steinbeck does not promise Paradise for the Joads. Their wildest dreams image not golden streets, but indoor plumbing. Dams will continue to break—babies will continue to be stillborn. But the people will go on: "this is the beginning—from 'I' to 'we.' " The grapes of wrath have ripened, and in trampling out the vintage the Dispossessed have committed themselves (like Casy) to die to make men free. In despair they learn the lesson; in wrath they share the rich red wine of hope.

WILLIAMS COLLEGE

• PROFESSOR WILLIAM E. TAYLOR *is the author of a play, COLONEL PHILLIPS; of a volume of poetry, MAN IN THE WIND; and teaches drama in the English department at Stetson University. He took his three degrees at Vanderbilt University, and taught there and at Lincoln Memorial University before coming to Stetson.*

Jennessee Williams: Academia On Broadway

ONE CRITICISM LEVELED at Tennessee Williams is that symbolism runs riot in his plays, indeed that he has recently been guilty of making his symbols real, hence, not realistic; or that he has become so interested in symbolic meaning that he has failed to undergird it with a naturalistic substructure with which a reader or an audience can identify. Certainly, the charge may not be leveled at Williams' two masterpieces, *The Glass Menagerie* and *A Streetcar Named Desire*. But it can be leveled at *Suddenly Last Summer*. Philip Hartung, for example, says (*The Commonweal*, Jan. 1, 1960), "One really doesn't believe *Suddenly Last Summer*, but neither does one quite disbelieve it—and the total effect is like that of a frightening nightmare that one can't shake off."

Henry Popkin, on the other hand, has defended Williams' symbolism (*Tulane Drama Review*, March, 1960) on the basis that Williams is not a "social" dramatist like, say, Arthur Miller; hence, his symbols have to work hard to convey meaning. There may be a questionable causal relationship here, which can be solved only if we know what Williams' themes are. It is obvious that Williams' favorite trick is to set up a conflict between a feminine decadent (usually a representative of Faulknerian Southern aristocracy) and a vital, if brutal, representative of the great unwashed, a Snopes-type character who is almost always a foreigner. *Streetcar*, it seems, should have satisfied his compulsion for this theme, for it is hard to see how that play could be improved upon.

However, Williams has played variations on it again and again. In *Suddenly Last Summer*, for example, there is Mrs. Venable, like Blanche DuBois older than she would like to be and certainly decadent enough, pitted against Dr. Cukrowicz, who, if not unwashed, is certainly vital. Furthermore, as Stanley Kowalski in *Streetcar* does to Blanche, Dr. Cukrowicz destroys his antagonist by revealing the truth which she wants hidden. In *Streetcar*, however, the hidden truth is fairly comprehensible. Blanche, far from being the spinster-lady schoolteacher she pretends to be, is a degenerate, if pitiable, nymphomaniac. What is Mrs. Venable's secret? Is it that her son Sebastian was eaten alive by a pack of wild Italian boys? That he was homosexual? The latter, certainly, though she insists he was "chaste." I suppose also the former. But the trouble is that there seems to be something *more*, something connected with the cannibal act. What is it?

We might find some help if we turn to one of the most sensational bits of dialogue in this sensational play, that description Mrs. Venable gives of her son's search for God in the Encantadas:

> We saw the great sea-turtles crawl up out of the sea for their annual egg-laying . . . Once a year. . . .
> The narrow beach, the color of caviar, was all in motion! But the sky was in motion too. . . .
> Full of flesh-eating birds and the noise of the birds, the horrible savage cries of the—

It goes on and it is, indeed, horrible. (As Eric Bentley has said, when Williams goes into his theory of the Awful, he's pretty awful.) Nevertheless, this, according to Mrs. Venable, is where Sebastian saw God, and it is clear that the Encantadas scene is a central symbol in *Suddenly Last Summer*. Its meaning seems fairly obvious: Nature red in tooth and claw.

Other symbols in the play have to do with the names of characters. Benjamin Nelson, in his critical biography of Williams, has pointed out that

> Just as the universe in *Suddenly Last Summer* is a devouring maw, its inhabitants—within the confines of this tale—all have names symbolic of organic life as if they too were intimately related to the jungle which lurks around them. Mrs. Venable's name is Violet; her attendant is named Mrs. Foxhill; Catherine, George and their mother are the Hollys; and Dr. Cukrowicz explains that his name in Polish means sugar.

If we add to this the insectivorous plants, the carnivorous birds, the mother who rejects her dying husband and keeps her son "chaste" (and dependent) by "satisfying" his demands, and the son himself, who describes men in terms of food, the total impression is appalling. Why, after all, should one be surprised that Sebastian is eaten alive? The problem, however, is not really why he is *eaten alive,* but why *he* is eaten alive. A look at further symbolic meanings in the names of characters in the play may help.

On a relatively simple level, the nun who is in charge of Catherine is called Sister Felicity, a name with ironic undertones considering the unpleasantness of her job and the feeling Catherine has for her. Mrs. Venable's last name, as well as her first, is suggestive. Again ironically, the word suggests "venerable," and Mrs. Venable is venerable only in so far as she is getting old. But according to the *N. E. D.* the word *venable* comes from the Latin root meaning *vendible,* "that which is sold or for sale," or "capable of being bought over or bribed; ready to lend support or exert influence for purely mercenary considerations; of an unprincipled and hireling character." And, of course, Mrs. Venable will give Dr. Cukrowicz the money for his experiments with lobotomies only if he will drill into Catherine's skull first. She has also bought and sold the Hollys and is holding out on them to be certain that they get Catherine to sign papers permitting the operation and don't themselves interfere. More significantly, Mrs. Venable, it turns out in the course of Catherine's narrative, has been a procurer of boys for Sebastian. The third definition in the *N. E. D.* is the one most applicable here: "connected or associated with sordid and unprincipled bargaining; subject to mercenary or corrupt influences." A final and different meaning of the word is this: "of blood; contained in the veins." Williams would like this definition because it would suggest his Laurentian notion that it is in the blood (meaning, as with Lawrence, genitals) that man *lives.*

Dr. Cukrowicz makes a point of calling attention to his name, if it hasn't already done so for itself. When he introduces himself to Mrs. Venable, she stumbles over the unpronounceable syllables. He simplifies for her: "Cu-kro-wicz. It's a Polish word that means sugar, so let's make it simple and call me Doctor Sugar." She takes him at his word and frequently calls him so from that point on. Since the Doctor knows the etymology of his name, perhaps we should. And we wonder about its significance. First, sugar is edible. Further, there is the fact that his kind of doctor is rather unpleasant. So Dr. Cukrowicz is sugar-coated. This might even explain that, unlike Stanley Kowalski, he is not unwashed. Merely for the sake of illustration, let me go again to the *N. E. D.,* where a very old quotation is cited as illustration of this application of the word: "Poyson, confected with sucre, is most piercing and deadlie." Dr. Cukrowicz is "piercing" enough when he performs his lobotomies, and even he is willing to admit that he is deadly:

> Well, it will be ten years before we can tell if the immediate benefits of the operation will be lasting or—passing or even if there'd still be—and this is what haunts me about it—any possibility, afterwards, of reconstructing a—totally sound person, it may be that the person will always be limited afterwards, relieved of acute disturbances but—*limited,* Mrs. Venable. . .

It is with Sebastian, however, that symbolism in *Sudden-ly Last Summer* is most revealing. In the movie version, the audience actually witnesses the cannibalism. In the play it is described in Catherine's narrative. Though even the narration makes great demands on the audience's ability to believe ("that willing suspension of disbelief for the moment that constitutes poetic faith" sometimes seems an inadequate phrase in the theater of Tennessee Williams), the movie version strains it to the point of breaking. As we have seen, the "devouring maw" symbolism should convince us that such cannibalism is believable. But it doesn't. Why? I believe the problem is with Sebastian, who is entirely too mysterious. What characterizing is done (in the play) is accomplished through the reporting of Mrs. Venable and Catherine —and they disagree. Indeed, their disagreement is the crux of the whole plot. How is it to be resolved? Typically, the movie version introduces a red herring in the love motif between Catherine and the doctor. As a playwright, Williams is a much better man than that. The play ends ambiguously: "I think we ought to at least consider the possibility that the girl's story could be true . . .," says the doctor. One thinks "My God, he gave her that truth serum. What more does he want?" And one answers, "Maybe Mrs. Venable's money." Williams, however, by leaving the truth of Catherine's narrative open to doubt, leaves, I believe, Sebastian's culpability open to doubt. Again, an answer may be found in Williams' choice of a name.

First, Mrs. Venable calls attention to Sebastian's name by telling Dr. Cukrowicz that Sebastian has a patron saint. So to *Butler's Lives of the Saints,* where (if we don't already know such things) we discover that St. Sebastian flourished under Diocletian, who, because the saint was instrumental in the martyrdom of others, "delivered him over to certain archers of Mauritania, to be shot to death." The orders were carried out, but St. Sebastian survived and was nursed back to health by a lady named Irene, whereupon St. Sebastian went to the Emperor and told him he was being too hard on Christians. "Recovering from his surprise, he [Diocletian] gave orders for him to be seized and beaten to death with cudgels, and his body thrown into the common sewer."

More to the point is another allusion in the name Sebastian. In the play, Sebastian is a poet, not an unusual occupation for a Williams hero. Furthermore, there is that garden full of exotic plants. Two other facts about Sebastian are interesting. First, his good looks are emphasized. This might merely be part of Williams' desire to make him unusual and interesting. It may reflect also the fact that St. Sebastian, according to the *Encyclopedia Brittanica*, "is a favorite subject of sacred art, being most generally represented undraped, and severely though not mortally wounded with arrows." One might, of course, infer sexual symbolism from the arrows, but the striking fact about Sebastian's good looks is that they are clearly related to his age. I wish to quote a bit of dialogue from the play to make what seems to me an important and interesting point.

Doctor:
Your son was young, Mrs. Venable?

Mrs. Venable:
Both of us were young, and stayed young, Doctor.

Doctor:
Could I see a photograph of your son, Mrs. Venable?

Mrs. Venable:
Yes, indeed you could Doctor. I'm glad that you asked to see one. I'm going to show you not one photograph but two. Here. Here is my son, Sebastian, in a Renaissance pageboy's costume at a masked ball in Cannes. Here is my son, Sebastian, in the same costume at a masked ball in Venice. These two pictures were taken twenty years apart. Now which is the older one, Doctor?

Doctor:
This photograph looks older.

Mrs. Venable:
The photograph looks older but not the subject. It takes character to refuse to grow old, Doctor—successfully to refuse to. . . .

Furthermore, in both the movie and the play, great emphasis is placed upon the image of Sebastian sitting in a sidewalk cafe. He is ill, both physically and mentally. When he leaves the cafe, he goes to his death.

It is perhaps by now apparent that Sebastian is not only a martyr but Sebastian Melnoth as well, the pseudonym Oscar Wilde used after he was released from prison and during his unhappy lonely exile in Europe. The insistence on Sebastian's unchanging youthful appearance in the two photographs suggests, at least to me, in spite of the reversal, Wilde's *The Picture of Dorian Gray* — if not a literal, a spiritual autobiography.

What is the purpose of this allusion? There are at least two that occur to mind instantly. First, there is the homosexuality. Second, there is the decadence. But more important than either of these is a third: the image of Oscar Wilde sitting alone in a European sidewalk cafe, deserted by his friends, derided by his public, and exiled from his nation—the *poete maudit, par excellence!* Here is the poet in the modern world, the man who sees God, however staggering the sight may be, degenerate, perverted, and deserted—finally devoured.

The cannibalism in *Suddenly Last Summer,* I conclude, is not merely sensational. It is symbolic of man's place in the "ravening maw" of nature. Williams is saying that men are no exception to the rule of life; they, like plants and animals, eat one another. It is no accident that Williams refuses to condemn Sebastian, for Sebastian is his hero. He is the poet, in whom the way of the world is transformed, misunderstood, and destroyed. Even Mrs. Venable is in a sense justified; bizarre as she is, she is nevertheless on the side of the saints in a world of merely wolfish mediocrity.

STETSON UNIVERSITY

• ELIOT D. ALLEN *took his degrees at Wesleyan University, Harvard, and Princeton. He has taught at the University of Virginia, the University of Massachusetts, and currently is at Stetson University.*

That Was No Lady... That Was Jack Kerouac's Girl

WHEN THE EXPLORERS from outer space are poking around amid the bomb-blasted ruins of our civilization and trying to reconstruct life in twentieth-century America, I hope that they do not base their ideas of our women exclusively on the novels of Mr. Jack Kerouac.

There are many aspects of post-World War II America about which Mr. Kerouac is as good and accurate an informant as any writer whose works the spacemen might find. Probably no one, for instance, could give them a better picture of the far west as seen from the freight car: the maze of tracks dim in the foggy night at the railroad yard, the passing flashes of station and town lights in the dark, the menacing railroad guards. Indeed, as far as cross-country travel goes, and especially travel of the free or cheap sort—hitchhiking, rod-riding, gasoline sharing in private cars, or even bus travel—Mr. Kerouac is the acknowledged prophet. His novel *On the Road* is the bible of such travel.

About jazz, too, Mr. Kerouac would be hard to beat, in any tempo. He gives us the music, the mad musicians, and the even madder people who crowd around to listen to them. In *On the Road* we see and hear a number of jam sessions:

> Out we jumped in the warm, mad night, hearing a wild tenorman bawling horn across the way, going 'EE-YAH! EE-YAH! EE-YAH!' and hands clapping to the beat and folks yelling, 'Go, go, go! . . .' The tenorman was blowing at the peak of a wonderfully satisfactory free idea, a rising and falling riff that went from 'EE-yah!' to a crazier 'EE-de-lee-yah!' and blasted along to the rolling crash of buttscarred drums hammered by a big brutal Negro with a bull neck who didn't give a damn about anything but punishing his busted tubs, crash, rattle-ti-boom, crash. Uproars of music and the tenorman *had* it, and everyone knew he had it. . . . They were all urging that tenorman to hold it and keep it with cries and wild eyes, and he was raising it up in a clear cry above the furor. A six-foot skinny Negro woman was rolling her bones at the man's hornbell, and he just jabbed it at her, 'Ee! ee! ee!'

And if we want to find out about the incredible beat parties in the "pads" of New York or San Francisco, again Mr. Kerouac is the man to tell us the truth—if not the whole truth, at least nothing but the truth.

> There were at least a hundred people in a basement apartment in the West Nineties. People overflowed into the cellar compartments near the furnace. Something was going on in every corner, on every bed and couch—not an orgy but just a New Year's party with frantic screaming and wild radio music. . . . Periodically we rushed out to the car to pick up more people. . . . Some of our newspaper friends came in from the office with bottles. . . . People were drawing pictures and drinking stale beer. I slept on a couch with a girl called Mona in my arms. Great groups filed in from the old Columbia Campus bar.

Despite all this virtuosity, however, there is one large area of life where I do not trust Mr. Kerouac. With all his wisdom and experience, he gives a strangely distorted picture of American women. Women wander in quantity through his books—important ones like Mardou Fox in *The Subterraneans;* Maggie, in *Maggie Cassidy;* Mary Lou in *On the Road;* and a host of others. They are almost all young. Except for Sal Paradise's aunt in *On the Road* and Mrs. Duluoz in *Dr. Sax,* we see very little of any older women, for Mrs. Martin in *Town and City* hardly counts. Mr. Kerouac's girls are almost all physically attractive. And taken all together, they are about as unrepresentative of the women of ordinary American life as they could be.

For one thing, they are singularly inarticulate. Actually, they do talk, but they rarely say anything. When they do, it is frequently abusive. One of the longer connected female speeches in Mr. Kerouac's novels occurs when, in *On the Road,* Galatea Dunkel calls down Dean Moriarty for neglecting his wife. In *Maggie Cassidy,* Maggie, taken for the first time to a college party in New York, spends most of a brief chapter in an intermittent monologue whose main thought is adequately summed up by her opening remark, "Jack, let's get out of here." Judie Smith, in *Town and City,* is full of charming sentiments: "Everybody clear out." "And that goes for you, Levinsky: you bring Waldo here once again and I'll kick you in the teeth." "I'm sick and tired of all you damn serfs." "Shaddap!"

We are told that Old Bull Lee's wife Jane talks at length:

> His relation with his wife was one of the strangest: they talked till late at night; Bull liked to hold the floor, he went right on in his dreary monotonous voice, she tried to break in, she never could; at dawn he got tired and then Jane talked and he listented snuffling and going *thfump* in his nose.

But if this is so, we are never privileged to hear one of these conversations.

One reason why Mr. Kerouac's women are so inarticulate is that they have no ideas, perhaps even no minds. Their lives are completely physical. While the men are "digging" the human scene around them, sitting far into the night discussing jazz or Zen Buddhism, the women operate on a different plane. They eat, drink, occasionally cook meals, make love, have babies, or sit waiting for their wandering men to return. Inez, Dean's third wife in *On the Road,* is the epitome of proper Kerouac female behavior:

Inez cooked in the kitchen and looked in with a wry smile. Everything was all right with her. 'Dig her? Dig her, man? That's Inez. See, that's all she does, she pokes her head in the door and smiles. Oh, I've talked with her and we've got everything straightened out most beautifully.'

In *The Dharma Bums,* Sean Monahan has the ideal wife,

a beautiful young honey-haired girl, her hair falling way down over her shoulders, who wandered around the house and yard barefooted hanging up wash and baking her own brown bread and cookies.

Of course, not all the girls are quite so gentle and cooperative. They can fight, too. In *On the Road,* the girl friend of a minor character named Damion takes exception to his behavior at a party, knocks him out with a roundhouse right to the jaw, and carries him home. Mardou Fox, the Negro girl in *The Subterraneans,* has a fist-fight with one of her male companions in which he is saved from being beaten only by the arrival of the police.

But if Mr. Kerouac's women are inarticulate verbally, they compensate by being uninhibited otherwise. Such a group of girls was never seen; but in his novels we see them, and we see all of them. Clothing is always being discarded. Our first introduction to a girl called Princess in *The Dharma Bums* takes place when Japhy "suddenly appeared at our little cottage with a pretty girl and came in and told her to take her clothes off, which she did at once." Later in the same book at a relatively respectable party at Sean Monahan's house, "the three couples took all their clothes off and danced a kind of quaint innocent polka hand-in-hand around the parlor." Mardou Fox runs naked through the streets of San Francisco at night. She is under psychiatric treatment, to be sure, and so we must make allowances. But what allowances are to be made for Mary Lou, who rides across several states in the front seat of a car with nothing on above her waist?

Undressing is only one aspect of the lack of inhibitions. Excessive drinking, of course, hardly needs to be mentioned. Drugs are an important part of the picture. Jane Lee consumes an estimated ten dollars' worth of benzedrine tubes per week. But she is less spectacular than Mary Lou:

> That night Mary Lou took everything in the books: she took tea, goofballs, benny, liquor, and even asked Old Bull for a shot of M, which of course he didn't give her: he did give her a martini. She was so saturated with elements of all kinds that she came to a standstill and stood goofy on the porch with me.

When we first meet Mardou Fox, it is at a party where she is sitting on the floor in front of an open newspaper on which "tea" is being rolled.

We are hardly surprised, too, that the girls who undress as often and as eagerly should make love with equal frequency and variety. One of the purple passages marked by college undergraduates in *On the Road* is the scene where Mary Lou is in bed with two men at once. In *The Dharma Bums*, Princess, who is not embarrassed at disrobing before strangers, is quite as willing to make love with them, consecutively, on the floor. In fact, love-making, as far as the girls in Mr. Kerouac's novels are concerned, is mostly just a good old indoor—or outdoor—sport, played in a spirit of good clean fun, with no holds barred and not many questions asked.

At the present moment, it seems likely that to future literary historians, Mr. Kerouac will remain, at the least, an interesting phenomenon of the mid century. In an article in the January, 1962, *Writer's Digest,* he says, "There can be no major writer without original genius." He is certainly original, and with his great energy and the productive years presumably still before him, he may develop into a major writer. Part of such development will have to include the discovery of more normal women, the kind of women that most of his readers have met and know about. Women are people, though Mr. Kerouac has yet to learn this fact. As it is, he may amuse or shock or frighten us, but he does not really enlighten us with any insight into the female half of the population.

When the spacemen begin writing up our civilization, I want them to understand that earthwomen were not like that at all—not really. Mary Lou and Mardou Fox and Jane Lee are not Miss—or Mrs.—America. As for me, if I have to put up with any of Mr. Kerouac's women, I'll take Sal Paradise's nice, respectable old aunt.

STETSON UNIVERSITY

• *Educated at the University of Illinois and Columbia University, R. P. ADAMS is now professor of English at Tulane University. He has taught at the University of Kentucky, Long Island University, Rutgers University, Lafayette College, and has been a Fulbright lecturer in France. Professor Adams' articles have appeared in many literary journals, such as PMLA,* AMERICAN QUARTERLY, AMERICAN LITERATURE, COLLEGE ENGLISH, *and* NEW ENGLAND QUARTERLY. *Recently, he collaborated with Roger Asselineau in translating the latter's* THE EVOLUTION OF WALT WHITMAN. *(Harvard University Press, 1960)*

James Gould Cozzens: A Cultural Dilemma

JAMES GOULD COZZENS has been called by one of his most enthusiastic admirers "a classic mind, operating in a romantic period." Another critic has said that, "In contrast with romantic optimists like Whitman and Emerson, Cozzens holds that human society is not only imperfect but inherently incapable of being perfected," and that his "picture of society is static in its implicit denial that change is equivalent to progress and the implied doubt that progress is possible at all." He has said about himself, "I am more or less illiberal, and strongly antipathetic to all political and artistic movements." The general view is that Cozzens is conservative rather than progressive, rational rather than emotional, realistic rather than sentimental, and classical rather than romantic.

It seems to me, however, that a close examination of Cozzens' work will lead to some questioning of this general view. For one thing—as critics have often noted—his most pervasive theme is change. In the romantic tradition generally, the most popular topic is the growth or development of a young person toward maturity. Cozzens has dealt with this topic, in perfectly obvious and conventional ways, in the series of short stories about Durham School which he published in the *Saturday Evening Post* in the 1930's, in *The Just and the Unjust*, in *Ask Me Tomorrow*, in *Michael Scarlett*, and in his first novel, *Confusion*. In these works there can be no question that Cozzens is in the main stream of the romantic tradition, at least so far as his theme is concerned.

He is less conventional, but perhaps no less romantic, in the fact that his protagonists are frequently not young but middle-aged. We quickly see that these relatively grown-up people are still subjected in various ways to change and to the need for change. They are faced with problems, accidents, emergencies that force them to take action, often in unaccustomed ways, or in ways that are unorthodox and inconsistent with their social and professional codes. It seems, in fact, that they are admirable and successful in more or less the degree that they are mavericks. Mr. Lecky in *Castaway*, a conformist if there ever was one, marooned in a department store, leads a miserable existence and apparently commits suicide. The sick and aging Captain Clendening in *S. S. San Pedro* is unable to cope with a rising emergency, and his subordinate officers, caught in a static framework of maritime discipline, are unable to take action to save either the ship or the passengers. Ernest Cudlipp, in *Men and Brethren,* is more successful and less conventional. He arranges for one of his spiritual charges to have an abortion, fails to prevent another from committing suicide, casts off another for hopeless unworthiness, and sends another back to a monastic vocation for which he is hardly fitted but without which he cannot live. Ernest suits his actions as well as he can to the circumstances he has to deal with; he compromises, hedges, and arranges, and in the end, though he feels far from noble, he survives and continues to be useful.

Dr. George Bull, in *The Last Adam,* is even more unorthodox. He practices medicine in a slipshod style, makes mistakes, fails to make calls, and is at least technically responsible for letting an epidemic of typhoid fever get started. However, it is also Dr. Bull who, at the suggestion of his old aunt and with the help of apparatus at the disposal of a younger and more conventionally scientific doctor, diagnoses the epidemic and has it brought under control. And it is plainly Dr. Bull, with his "good greedy vitality," his roaring energy, his unpredictable outbreaks, and his informal but effective resourcefulness, that Cozzens would have his readers admire, not the respectable leading citizens of the town who try unsuccessfully to get him barred from practice. The implication of these instances is reasonably clear, I think. Although no man is perfect, the relatively good man is the one who deals, responsibly and effectively, with a changing situation. The less good man is unable to keep ahead of things; he fails to shift or change fast enough to control his changing environment, or his relation to it, and he is likely to be destroyed by it.

In his two most recent novels, *Guard of Honor* and *By Love Possessed,* Cozzens continues to develop the same dynamic implications. Colonel Ross, the chief center of awareness in *Guard of Honor,* is a good man. Like Ernest Cudlipp, he deals more or less effectively with a tangle of unexpected problems and difficulties. By ingenuity and by compromise, which sometimes looks like compromise of principle, he keeps an air base organization from breaking down during a short period when the commanding officer, General Beal, seems to be abdicating his responsibilities. In the end, however, it appears that General Beal, who resembles Dr. Bull in some ways, is an even better man, at least for the basic purposes of war, than Colonel Ross. Though he seems naive and immature in dealing with administrative situations, we gather that he is an excellent battle commander. He is the youngest general officer in the Army, and he is slated for a major overseas command when the big air-ground assault on Europe is launched. When he does take up his responsibilities, he has a firm hand. "By God," he says, "I think I'll shake this place up! . . . We're going to get rid of some dead wood—" Colonel Ross has been worried about the visit of General Nichols, a staff officer from Washington, who has evidently come to see how General Beal is doing. General Beal is much less concerned. "Don't worry, Judge," he says,

> even Jo-Jo knows they could do without him before they could do without me. That's not boasting, Judge. There's a war on. Jo-Jo can talk to Mr. Churchill; but the war, that's for us. Without me—without us, he wouldn't have a whole hell of a lot to talk about, would he?

The point is that those who control or direct or suppress the energies and capabilities of men, however useful such administrative labors may be, are less important, after all, than those who embody the energies and whose creative power makes the whole apparatus of a war, or of society in general, move. To put it another way, those who cause change are more important than those who only meet it and to some extent successfully control or guide it.

By Love Possessed has most often been interpreted as being "about" the Man of Reason beset and sometimes overcome by passion. But the usual implication, that reason should prevail and passion be suppressed, is not entirely borne out by the evidence in the text. In the first place, it is not Arthur Winner, the central character, who is called the Man of Reason, but his dead father, Arthur Winner Senior. In the second place, the notion attributed to Arthur Winner, Senior concerning "love's bliss of thoughtlessness" is this: "Love pushed aside the bitter findings of experience. Love knew for a fact what was not a fact; with ease, love believed the unbelievable; love wished and made it so." From which he is said to have concluded, not that love is undesirable, but rather that the opposite view is at least possible. "Moreover, here where love's weakness seemed to be, love's strength resided. Itself all unreality, love was assailed by reality in vain." The flavor of the ridiculous that informs this pronouncement derives from both sides of the ironic contradiction: reason, so widely touted as man's most effective tool for dealing with reality, is actually a much less potent—though admittedly also less dangerous—weapon than love, or passion.

Arthur Winner the son has this contradiction brought home to him in many ways, chiefly by being made to think about two crucial matters: his own brief but violent love affair with Marjorie, the wife of his partner and close friend Julius Penrose; and the fact, which he discovers at the end of the story, that his other partner, old Noah Tuttle, is in some sense an embezzler. Julius, who has known these things for years without ever having said a word about either of them, advises Arthur Winner to keep the same close counsel. The logic of his position seems unorthodox, but, given his premises and the circumstances, it is convincing. Noah Tuttle has control of several trust funds involving large amounts of money. Years ago he has given poor guidance to some of his clients by advising them to invest in an interurban railroad company, which has gone bankrupt. Noah has undertaken to liquidate its assets, and has managed to repay the investors much more than anyone expected. What Arthur Winner now discovers is that he has done so by juggling other funds. What Julius points out is that Noah is slowly but, so far, surely making up the shortage. No one has been injured; many have benefited. Nothing is to be gained, and much will be lost, if the fraud is exposed. Therefore, in order to protect Noah, himself, and Julius, and do the most good for Noah's clients, Arthur Winner must conceal his knowledge of the unorthodox dealing and, from now on, aid and abet it in any way he can.

This, as one good critic has pointed out, is pragmatism. Cozzens is saying, in effect, that ideas, including moral ideas, and even when they are embodied in law, are not valid *a priori*. They are validated by experience, judged, as we say, by their results in action. They have no eternal, absolute sanction in God or in the nature of things. Everything is relative; everything changes; every decision must be made in the context of the situation in which it is required; every action must be planned to meet the circumstances in which its effects will be felt. This is moral relativism, which must logically be based on metaphysical dynamism. It is the very opposite of a static philosophy. It is not classical; it is modern; it has come into prominence with the development of the romantic tradition. It is an aspect of modern thinking to which our few surviving classically conservative minds object most vehemently and, from the point of view of their tradition, most properly. On the basis of these thematic materials, therefore, it seems to me clear that Cozzens cannot be regarded as a classical conservative. Thematically, he is a pretty thorough and consistent romantic.

In other respects, however, Cozzens is not so romantic. His inconsistency in this can be illustrated by further reference to *By Love Possessed*. The original intention of that novel, according to a letter from Cozzens to his editor in 1950, was to present "a conflict between the works of human thinking and the works of human feeling," and the crisis was to turn on "my lawyer's difficulty in imagining what can possess his wife in slowly going Catholic." Philosophically, the conflict was to be between "the Law's rational design to have the facts" and "the usually triumphant emotional wish . . . to down mere 'facts' and to rise over them by a different logic where feeling counts as Higher Knowing." Or, we might say roughly, between classical and romantic ways of arriving at decisions. He went on,

> I have to acknowledge that I work under a limitation here in that such Knowing is utterly beyond me; yet I think it is true when I say I have no hostile feelings and no wish to deride what I do not understand; on the contrary, seeing it as I see it, I find it affecting—an example of the general wishful human persistence in make-believe. Naturally I will deal only with what I am able to know, which is the cold dismay or unhappy amazement which those whose minds can get no

higher than the Law's level of common sense must find themselves experiencing when they come up against the goings-
on whose origin is spiritual. . . .

In the final outcome, *By Love Possessed* has been made
to transcend this supposed limitation by a fairly wide mar-
gin, as we have seen. But the problem is real and important, because the theme or fact of change is logically involved
with feeling and emotion. If we are primarily and per-
vasively interested in the effects of change, as Cozzens is in
all his works, then we can hardly help having to deal sympathetically, or better empathetically, with the forces that
really move us; and these are much more closely associated
with feeling or emotion than they are with fact or logic.
Desire is irrational; we want what does not exist and what
we do not need; and facts do give way; things change; men
change. The classical world is dead. The modern world
is dynamic, relativistic, and romantic, in spite of "the cold
dismay or unhappy amazement" of some. A writer of fiction
has to believe in make-believe, and he has to make the reader believe, in order to weave a web of passion-spun plot and
make a story of it, and he has to deal in some way effectively
with emotion as the main basis of the action. The critical
difficulty, for me, with Cozzens is that he has adopted the
theme of change but has never been sufficiently able to commit himself to methods that would make that theme come
fully alive.

The resulting inadequacy might be most conveniently
indicated by the relative lack of pressure or high intensity
in Cozzens' work. Any fundamental change, in an individual's personality, or in his environment, or in his relation
to other people or things—or in all of these together, since
in practice they generally do all come together—is really a
soul-shaking experience. It cannot be treated lightly or ab-
stractly. It is by nature intense, charged with extremes of
hope and fear, triumph or despair—always with emotion of
great complexity, force, and urgency. If it is to be treated
realistically and adequately, this urgency, this overpowering

intensity of the energy actually involved in change, must be conveyed with appropriate power in the writing.

Cozzens has not, to any great extent, made use of the literary resources developed in the romantic tradition for the purpose of rendering this kind of powerful feeling. His style is essentially eighteenth-century, like that of Swift or Steele, both of whom he admires. It is good for saying that whatever is, is right (or wrong, as the case may be), but it is not so good for saying that whatever is, is continually changing. He does not use the symbolic structure of death and rebirth which many romantics from Wordsworth to Hemingway have used to formulate the essence of change, nor does he use the kind of symbolic imagery with which they commonly reinforce that structure and that theme. As a result, his heroes tend to give an impression of stuffiness or priggishness instead of the vision of heroic maturity arising out of heroic struggle which they seem to be intended to give. They and the works they live in are, to a degree, intellectually abstract and emotionally thin.

The best way I can think of to illustrate this opinion is to compare Cozzens' work to that of William Faulkner, who also deals with the theme of change and who fully acknowledges the difficulty, uncertainty, and fearsomeness of change. I have been reading both for several months, and have found that for my taste Cozzens suffers severely by the comparison. Faulkner uses myth, symbolism, metaphor, time distortion, synesthesia, kinesthesia, oxymorons, twisted syntax, marathon sentences, and dozens of other conventional and unconventional devices to put across his enormous feeling for the intensity of life; and he succeeds. Cozzens presents a smoother surface and a blander texture, and the result, for me, is that his picture does not convince. This is not the quality of life as I have known it. This does not get where I have been among the guts and tough tendons of things.

This is not to say that I dislike Cozzens or that I think him a bad writer. He is a very good one, whose work I always enjoy reading; but he is not, as I believe Faulkner is, among the very great. The inconsistency between his theme and his method seems to me to weaken his results.

Let me recapitulate briefly, by way of conclusion, what this inconsistency is and how it relates to the two traditions which it seems to me Cozzens is straddling. It is misleading, I think, to call him "a classic mind," or a conservative, or a celebrator of static values and let it go at that. Intellectually, he is convinced that change is universal, necessary, and inevitable; and in this respect he belongs squarely in the romantic tradition of dynamic relativism, or pragmatism. At the same time he appears to be temperamentally or, if you like, emotionally inclined to wish that these things were not so. Instead of being "a classic mind, operating in a romantic period," I regard him rather as a romantic mind unable to divorce itself from a classic temperament. The critic of his work must, I feel, respect both its intellectual insistence on the need for change and its emotional discomfort in the face of change. Such conflicts are probably, on the whole, good for art. But the greatest works of modern art, including the art of fiction, if I am not mistaken, do not come out of exactly this kind of conflict, but rather out of a conflict between an intense desire for fundamental change and the resistance that any effort to bring about such change must always encounter. Cozzens has, in a sense, turned this conflict upside down, has put his head where his heart ought to be, and deprived his work of the kind of power that Faulkner, for example, achieves.

TULANE UNIVERSITY

• DR. WARREN FRENCH *is the author of* JOHN STEIN-
BECK, FRANK NORRIS, *and* J. D. SALINGER, *three critical
studies published by Twayne. His poems and articles
have appeared in various magazines and journals. Taking his doctorate at the University of Texas, Professor
French has taught at Stetson University, the University
of Florida, and is now at Kansas State University.*

The Quaking

World of

James Purdy

BACK IN '58 WHEN Frederick
Gwynn and Joseph Blotner beat
other literary lawmen to the draw
with the trail-breaking book about
J. D. Salinger, they allowed—dead
on target—that "the only Post-War
fiction unanimously approved by contemporary literate
American youth" was about five-hundred pages by the author
of *The Catcher in the Rye*. Times have changed. Just as this
notice was being circulated, a stranger to be reckoned with
rode into town. No other word-slinger since Salinger has
made as much impression upon contemporary collegians as
middle-thirtyish Midwesterner James Purdy.

One would hope that American writers would no longer
need to go abroad for recognition, but when Purdy began
circulating his short stories, he — like many distinguished
predecessors—found no native takers. Staking himself to a
privately printed book, he was warmly received in England
and commercially published at home only after British critics (led by Edith Sitwell) had praised the exciting novelty
of his work.

*This essay is revised and greatly expanded from an introduction to Purdy in the first
issue of *Scope*, the University of Florida literary magazine.

I was startled when a perceptive friend of mine abroad wrote that Purdy's first novel *Malcolm* struck him as "degenerate." I had never thought of it as that; but the fact that I hadn't may be simply a deplorable symptom that Americans are beginning to accept as normal the loveless state of affairs in which talk is incessant but communication non-existent. While there are few signs of truly human feeling anywhere today, elsewhere the educated may bear less resemblance than Americans to Purdy's Fenton Riddleway, who "was able to accept nearly anything . . . the immense dreariness of things as though there were no other possibility."

The surrealistic world of *Malcolm* is degenerate, but what has made the novel popular is not that it makes this grotesque world appealing, but that it shocks readers into recognizing that it is unmistakably theirs. It is a vastly different matter whether a book's degeneracy results from the writer's offering an enticing escape from reality (as in *Gone With the Wind* or *Lady Chatterley's Lover* or *On The Road*) or from his attempting to make us face unpleasant realities (as in *Suddenly, Last Summer* or *Cards of Identity* or *The Sound and the Fury*).

While it would be unjustifiably cruel to deprive addicts of tranquilizers like the first group of books, the permanent value of literature lies in the second. If such works, however, merely present a degenerate state, like Genet's plays or John Updike's novels, they are not likely to be of any more enduring value than the vast bulk of abstract expressionist paintings that perform the same useful but limited function visually. The question to be asked of any author is, does he recognize our world for what it is while remaining able to perceive the possibility of some improvement upon it? Purdy's significance is that when we ask this question about him, we can answer—as we can of few authors—"Yes."

The novelist himself has been quoted in the *Library Journal* as saying that "people are losing their character as real people." As his most perceptive reviewer, William

Peden, correctly asserts in an early appraisal in the *Saturday Review*, Purdy writes of a world of "unbearable loneliness." He is concerned, like many contemporary writers, with attempts to establish communication in a hostile, hysterical world, a quaking world that seems about to fragment under intolerable pressures of suspicion and selfishness into a million jagged, meaningless pieces.

A key to his work is "Why Can't They Tell You Why?," one of the few short stories that is genuinely frightening in this age of meretricious horror. The story describes a small boy's sickening defeat in his attempt to cling to reminders of a lost father, in the face of malicious persecution from a mother who refuses to accept her role because she does not wish to admit she is aging.

I do not think Purdy has borrowed the theme of the search for a father from literary sources. While he must be familiar with the persistence of the Telemachus motif in Western literature, particularly its embodiment in the monumental experimental writings of James Joyce, he need not have turned to books for inspiration; he need only have observed the millions of broken homes and thoughtless parents sullying our society to find the material for his poignant fiction.

The theme recurs often in *Color of Darkness*, the first collection of Purdy's short stories. In the title story, although the father is alive and the mother dead, he is so often "away," so involved in being a "success" at the work that is the only thing that has "real meaning" for him, that his young son's attempting to swallow the father's wedding ring and kicking the man "vigorously in the groin" are not simply desperate gestures, but startling symbols of his resentment of being born.

The melancholy consequences of the alienation of father and son are most skillfully depicted in "Cutting Edge," which concerns a selfish couple named Zeller, "who had learned nothing from life, were stopped and drifting where they were twenty years before." Their son puts into words what many of Purdy's other characters cannot when he tells his father, "You never wanted anything from me and you never wanted to give me anything. I didn't matter to you." When the son visits the parents in Florida, "a stranger who despised them," wearing a beard that offends his mother and sunbathing in the nude to show "his nakedness to both of them," he forces them to recognize that "the fruit of their lives and the culmination of their twenty years" is the "glacial control that had come to him out of art and New York."

Many of Purdy's characters do not achieve even the Joycean "epiphany" granted the highly verbal Zellers but continue rather to live, in Thoreau's famous phrase, "lives of quiet desperation," trying like Mrs. Farebrother in "Sound of Talking," "to think what she *did* want" and finding that "one thing or another or nothing were all the same."

What these people do unconsciously want is best summed up in a statement from *The Catcher in the Rye* that links Salinger and Purdy as observers of a distraught society. Describing the exhibits at the Museum of Natural History, Holden Caulfield says that "the best thing . . . in the museum was that everything always stayed right where it was. Nobody'd move." The unwilling mothers, the indifferent fathers continually shun change and destroy their children's youth in order to preserve their own.

Purdy's clearest exposition of this truly "unnatural" resistance to change is a short story that has often been mistakenly regarded as merely humorous, "Plan Now to Attend." Mr. Graitop, who has introduced the "new Religion" to America, has succeeded in arresting change. When he is undressed after passing out, an observer is astounded to discover that this "man of at least forty . . . looked like a boy of sixteen . . . a youth untouched by life and disappointment." But he has bought this immunity to the human condition at the expense of complete alienation from society. Although a successful soul-saver, even his ex-college roommate addresses him as "Mister" and tells him that "nobody ever even really liked you." The frustrating search for a father goes on because people refuse to age as a father must or to accept their own humanity as they must before they can accept anyone else's.

Lack of feeling is the reason why the "Dead" people in "63: Dream Palace" pay "absolutely no attention . . . perhaps to anything." If they are not completely preoccupied in their own trivial pursuits, the truth may break through to them. Only the "excessive" boy from West Virginia, who experiences the break with the past that comes when those truly dear to him actually die, escapes the alcoholic living death of the others and leaves behind a tale to console them on their "bad nights."

This first of Purdy's longer fictions is not entirely satisfactory. The story is a collection of the picaresque fragments of a heroic history that an aimless writer invents for his effete friends about a boy who has the vitality to accept life. The device of the tale-within-a-tale does not work well, however, because—as might be anticipated—the primitive Fenton Riddleway, who wished to see dead "the only two people he had loved in the world," runs away with the story. Since Purdy overlooked some dangers of making the phantom more real than the people who invented him, to compensate for their own inadequacies, the alternate naiveté and sophistication of Fenton's conversation and the unsupported speculations about his fate distract from the impact of this tale about people who have already ceased to be real.

Purdy overcomes these difficulties in *Malcolm* by dispensing with an internal narrator and writing an unapologetically fantastic story in the form of a traditional success story to sum up the trenchant criticisms of the world that he had been making so far.

Malcolm has baffled critics because they have failed to recognize that it is perhaps the first employment in fiction of a distinctively surrealistic style that does not attempt to imitate the devices of surrealistic painting in an uncongenial medium, but does attempt to employ analogous devices

suited to the different medium. Most attempts at literary
surrealism have come to grief because they have been un-
intelligible, when read simply as stories; but *Malcolm*, read
without regard for an underlying meaning, is like a high-
spirited trip through Freedomland, designed to sate the
fancy of those who love fast movement and immediate
sensation. It is a kind of modern *Alice in Wonderland* that
one can enjoy simply for the fertility of the author's zany
imagination. *Malcolm* proves, however, that a kaleidoscopic
whirl of impressions need not be merely the dope-addict's
dream that much Beat writing like *Naked Lunch* is. Purdy
achieves the rare combination of madness and method.

The convoluted plot of *Malcolm* concerns the decline
and fall of a teen-ager abandoned by his father at "one of
the most palatial hotels in the world." Picked up by an
ambitious astrologer who provides him with a set of "addresses," Malcolm ages prematurely as he is received and exploited by as grotesque a group of characters as any novelist
has invented. Finally he is wed to a nymphomaniacal night-
club singer, because "too young for the army, too unpre-
pared to continue his schooling and become a scientist, too
untrained for ordinary work—what was left for him but
marriage?" And marriage "which ushers most people into
life . . . ushered him into happiness—and death," since he
dies of "sexual hyperaesthesia" brought on by satisfying the
demands of his wife who comes home only to taste "every
joy of marriage . . . though rapidly, to the full." After his
death, a rumor circulates that "there had been no corpse at
all," that "nobody was buried in the ceremony."

Too much significance can be read into the last statement. Purdy is not interested in creating some kind of supernatural mystery, but is stressing that Malcolm is not a real
individual—he is a haunting symbol of the position of youth
in a self-seeking, materialistic society. As William Peden
points out, the novel is a "compelling allegory" of a world
in which "youth and innocence are destroyed."

Purdy's point seems to be like Paul Goodman's in *Grow-*

ing Up Absurd—that we have provided our youth with every advantage except love and a sense of dignity. We surround adolescents with luxuries, but deny them the guidance that they deserve so that they fall into the hands of charlatans. A close link between the novel and Purdy's early short stories is provided by Malcolm's remark that his vanished father seemed "to feel I was always going to stay just the way I was."

I do not think it is necessary to assign a specific symbolism to each of the fantastic creatures Malcolm meets in his premature travels—Estel Blanc, Kermit and Laureen Raphaelson, the imposing Girards, the Contemporaries—to make the point that none provides him with the affectionate guidance he needs. ("I suppose if somebody would tell me what to do, I would do it," Malcolm says as he starts down the road to disaster.) All seek rather to exploit his youth and innocuous charm—to "use" him as Fenton Riddleway charged Parkhearst Cratty might. As a result Malcolm is reduced to the level of a beast, good for nothing but to be branded (in the tattooing scene during which he no longer even feels pain) and put at stud until he is worn out. Beneath the wild humor, *Malcolm* attacks relentlessly a society that knows only physical values. The absence of a corpse means only that once this society has used a person up, it is done with him—or perhaps that even the society exists only in its own sick fancies. Both the character and the world he moves in may be simply hallucinatory.

An indication of Purdy's stature is his refusal to stop experimenting. Few experimental novels are popular enough to become inexpensive paperbacks, and success might have tempted Purdy—as it has other recent writers—to keep expressing over and over his irrefutable points about society's destruction of youth. His career could as easily have exemplified the law of diminishing returns as those of Norman Mailer or Calder Willingham or Kingsley Amis if he had been content to put the same freaks through their fantastic paces time after time. It is a relief and a happy omen to find that his second novel, *The Nephew,* differs vastly in both style and tone from his first and yet is at least its equal. How many authors recently have followed a good first novel with a good second?

That something was brewing is evident from some short stories that appeared in *Commentary* and *Partisan Review* in 1959 even before *Malcolm* hit the bookstores. "Everything Under the Sun," "Encore," and "Mrs. Benson" are quite different from any of Purdy's previous writings. They mark a return to the realism of his earlier short stories, but they display also a new and more mature sense of compassion. All are concerned with problems of identity. "You need me *to tell you who you are,*" fifteen-year-old Cade tells his friend Jesse in "Everything Under the Sun," the best of these stories, and he speaks for many of Purdy's recent brainchildren. The story itself foreshadows the much more delicately traced subplot in *The Nephew* about Willard Baker's neurotic dependence on Vernon Miller.

Jesse in the short story has taken in the younger brother of an Army buddy who died saving his life, but he is not satisfied to accept the boy as he is. "Ever since you give up women and drinking you been picking on me," Cade tells him. Jesse has also started going to the Jesus Saves Mission; but at the climax of the story, Cade, by threatening to leave, forces Jesse to accept him as he is and to give up the Mission. Purdy here asserts what he has intimated earlier—that we cannot find happiness by fleeing from the natural into the supernatural or by refusing to accept people as we find them. The failure of most human relationships is summarized by a doctor in "Encore," when he tells his sister, who has been complaining about her son:

> 'You're old and tired and complaining, and because you can't put your finger on what's wrong, you've decided that there's something wrong with your son because he goes, of all places, to a Greek restaurant and talks to Spyro, who draws rather well and who is now making a picture of your son.'

The failure of communication is a recurrent theme in

Purdy's work. What is new in these short stories is that he does hold out in their ambiguous endings a possibility of hope. In "Everything Under the Sun," the threatened break is averted and the younger boy once more exposes his tattoo that is identical to his friend's; in "Encore," although the mother and son cannot weep together, she tells him finally to keep playing the harmonica for her. Although the road is not clear, there may be a way out of the jungle of self.

This new attitude of compassion distinguishes *The Nephew*. The theme here is the same as in much of Purdy's earlier work: the nephew, who never appears in the story, has been a drifter in a fatherless world. The lack of communication in our society is nowhere more clearly revealed than in the statement that the aunt who is compiling a memorial to the boy she has reared has never really known him. Like *Malcolm, The Nephew* occurs in a superficial world where people impinge upon each other without having the most elementary sense of each others' individuality. The two are even specifically linked by the "burned saccharine smell" of cooking ketchup that overwhelms the scent of roses at Malcolm's funeral and pervades the little town in *The Nephew* during dull, sultry summer days.

The second novel is, although less diverting, even more gripping than *Malcolm* because it takes place not in a weary wonderland but in an expertly pictured middle-class neighborhood in a typical American town, ironically named Rainbow Center, that is frighteningly reminiscent of not only Purdy's native Ohio River Valley but of almost any place in the United States where people like Maud in "A Good Woman" live on mud and dreams.

The Nephew also differs in tone from its predecessor. The unseen title character is not the guiltless victim of a degenerate society, for as another character points out, Cliff was "too proud to admit he needed love from anybody . . . too proud to think anyone felt they wanted to love him." He made the same error as Jesse in "Everything Under the Sun." Although he is now lost beyond recall on a Korean battlefield, and the tattered souvenirs of his past—like his aunt and uncle's old flag—are beyond recovery, some qualified happiness is predicted for others in the story. Although one of the characters observes that the central failure—of never knowing those closest to us—is "universal," the long exploited Vernon Miller and Faye Laird and even Cliff's aunt and uncle—after being physically and mentally battered —have learned at last to admit that they need love enough to break down the walls of selfish pride that isolate those who need each other.

Purdy, like most significant artists, is an innovator within a tradition. Just as *Malcolm* depends for part of its effectiveness on its wistful satire of the Dickensian novel, *The Nephew*—which mentions but minimizes alcoholism, adultery and worse—ridicules the sensational best-sellers about small towns (like *Kings Row* and *Peyton Place*) that stress the superficially scandalous but miss the real tragedy of a community in which, as one of the characters puts it, "we're all pretty much strangers to one another."

Purdy's work also belongs to the even older tradition of the debate between the body and the soul, expressing an attitude much like Whitman's in "Song of Myself":

> I have said that the soul is not more than the body
> And I have said that the body is not more than the soul,
> And nothing, not God, is greater to one than one's self is,
> And whoever walks a furlong without sympathy walks to his
> funeral drest in his shroud.

Purdy turns his withering wit upon a degenerate society that seeks only physical sensation and that in its quest for perpetual youth destroys what it seeks, but he blasts also with mordant scorn those haters of life who seek to be "all soul." He sees that the ancient search for the father will be satisfied only when man accepts gracefully the fact of his own maturing and aging and his responsibility for giving the promise of youth the affectionate guidance that might enable it to fulfill itself. His contemptuous view of those who sit waiting for others to do what they should themselves is best summarized in his remarkable "Sermon" in New Directions annual No. 17.

Purdy holds out little hope of improvement and none of miraculous cure, but his expression of faint hope for the enlightenment of the afflicted is far more realistically positive than the spun-sugar fantasies of "popular" writers and is actually far less escapist than the lamentations of those "realists" resigned to wallowing in degeneracy. There is a dream world even in *The Nephew,* but the dream is no longer all nightmare as in Purdy's earlier works.

This dream, though, is neither pointless weeping over what may never have been nor fatuous promise of pie in the sky. It is the kind of dream that those who cannot ignore the degeneracy of the contemporary world may be able to accept when they must reject worn-out banalities paraded as ideals—the kind of dream that cannot stop a world of unremitting change from quaking, but that might prevent its shattering by giving people the vision to move with it. It will be interesting to see where Purdy himself moves in his next novel. If it resembles its predecessors, it will bring to a world loaded with pleasant trivia and dull morality a rare combination of delight and edification.

Kansas State University

This book was set in BASKERVILLE and THOMPSON QUILL SCRIPT.

It was printed and bound by CONVENTION PRESS, Jacksonville, Florida.

Design by TRUMAN PENDARVIS